W9-BKI-092

Contents

Acknowledgments

We would like to thank our editors at New Harbinger Publications—Tesilya Hanauer, Heather Mitchener, and Jasmine Star—for their support and assistance in the preparation of this book. We are grateful as well to Laura Miller, MD, and Radmilla Manev, MD, who read early drafts and provided valuable feedback on ways to improve the content of this text.

We also owe much to the researchers who have dedicated their careers to better understanding and treating anxiety. Among those responsible for developing and studying the treatments outlined in this book are David H. Barlow, Thomas D. Borkovec, Aaron T. Beck, Michel J. Dugas, Robert Ladouceur, Adrian Wells, Richard G. Heimberg, and Michelle G. Craske.

Finally, and above all else, we would like to thank our patients, who have taught us just as much as we have taught them about overcoming anxiety.

Introduction

Tell people you're writing a book about worry and the reaction is almost always the same: "I need a copy!" Of course, if you are writing a book about worry, that's exactly what you want to hear. But this response also highlights the pervasiveness of worry in today's world. In fact, we truly live in an era of worry. Ours is a time filled with the ominous sense that danger lurks around every corner. And it's not just the dramatic, newsworthy threats that concern us—it's our daily lives. We worry about our finances, our health, our relationships, and our children. In fact, we even worry about how much we worry!

Maybe we should. If you suffer from excessive, uncontrolled worry, you already know that it can cause significant problems. Chronic worriers suffer from physical symptoms, such as headaches, backaches, upset stomachs, and insomnia. Close relationships become distant and strained, marked by arguing, irritability, and withdrawal. Alcohol use increases, and other mental disorders, such as depression or panic disorder, can develop. Productivity at work declines, procrastination takes hold, and pleasant activities, such as exercising or dining out, are shelved. Excessive worry truly affects all areas of life.

Fortunately, there's hope. *10 Simple Solutions to Worry: How to Calm Your Mind, Relax Your Body, and Reclaim Your Life* specifically targets the problem of excessive worry. Using the research-proven methods of cognitive behavioral therapy

(CBT), this book is a prescription for those who worry too much. Inside, you'll find a concise guide that describes core CBT strategies for controlling worry. We carefully chose these strategies because of their powerful impact on worry.

Despite the tenacity of worry, research shows that the strategies presented here can be remarkably effective. For example, a study by Thomas Borkovec compared CBT and relaxation techniques to a more traditional therapeutic approach. The study found that those with chronic worry showed the greatest improvement when treated with either relaxation strategies or CBT (Borkovec and Costello 1993). Another study, by Robert Ladouceur and his colleagues, showed that cognitive behavioral treatment of worry using strategies similar to those described in this book, such as worry exposure and accepting uncertainty, was also effective in treating chronic worry (Ladouceur, Dugas, et al. 2000).

We can also attest to the value of these techniques because we use them every day in our own practices. In fact, we've used each step described in this book to help hundreds of patients learn to control worry. And we keep using these strategies because they work.

We're excited to bring you these cutting-edge techniques. In our daily work, we frequently hear that CBT for worry isn't widely available. Regrettably, despite the rapid growth of CBT in the past few decades, that's often true—even in a major city like Chicago, where we practice. We wrote this book to help bridge that gap and offer you the same tools that our patients find so helpful. Our hope is that with these tools you too can experience life without unproductive worry.

How to Use This Book

As you read through this book, you'll notice each chapter contains two parts. First, we describe a specific technique for controlling worry. Then we offer several self-help exercises so you can practice applying the technique to your worry. We included these self-help exercises because they are *essential* to your success. If you truly want to learn to control your worry, it's important to complete the exercises. Overcoming worry requires time and effort. It's crucial to pick up a pen and a piece of paper—just like our patients do—and get to work.

In addition to completing the self-help exercises, you'll receive maximum benefit from this book if you follow these tips:

- Keep this book with you. It's designed to be portable so you can work on mastering your worry whenever it strikes.

- Get a notebook specifically for completing the self-help exercises.

- Use this book as an adjunct to therapy. Self-help and therapy often work well together. If you are currently in therapy for worry, working through the steps in this book can help speed your progress along.

- Reward yourself for your efforts. Change is difficult. You deserve something for all of your hard work. It may be something small like dessert or something big like a vacation. Either way, reward yourself for working so hard to overcome your worry.

We wish you luck in your quest to control your worry. In our practices, we witness firsthand the benefits of learning to manage worry. We see joy, happiness, peace, and productivity return to our patients' lives. We hope this book will bring you the same benefits.

1

Understand Worry

Understanding worry can be elusive and challenging at times—even for psychologists and therapists. In this chapter, we'll take the mystery out of worry by clearly defining it, explaining the difference between productive and unproductive worry, and describing the four main ways worry affects you. We'll also introduce you to self-monitoring, a technique that will help you understand—and control—your own worry.

What Is Worry?

Amazingly, despite being a universal human experience, worry has proven remarkably difficult to clearly define (Mennin, Heimberg, and Turk 2004). Only recently have researchers developed a clear understanding of worry. From intensive study of people who worry excessively, we now know that an accurate definition of worry consists of three key parts: future orientation, catastrophizing, and language-based thoughts.

The first essential component of worry is a *future orientation*. In other words, when you worry you invariably focus on something that might happen but hasn't happened yet. This notion may seem a bit controversial. In fact, you might even disagree with it. You might argue that you worry about things that are happening *right now*, not in the future. A closer look, though, reveals the truth—worry is like a haunted crystal ball, tormenting you with a terrifying view of the future.

Let's look at an example. Suppose you're on your way to an important meeting when you suddenly get a flat tire. As a result, you feel anxious, stressed, and worried. However, before you assume that it's your current predicament that's got you worried, ask yourself this question: Is your worry really about the flat tire? Or are you worried about the potential consequences of the flat tire? If you feel worried, your mind is almost certainly racing with thoughts of the future consequences. You might think, "How much is this going to cost? What happens if I'm late for that important meeting? I could've been killed—are my tires even safe? Now I'll probably have to cancel my date for tonight." As you can see, when worry strikes—even during an actual negative event such as a flat tire—it inflicts pain by looking to the future for disasters that haven't yet happened.

Of course, merely focusing on the future doesn't fully capture the essence of worry. After all, a positive view of the future can make you feel hopeful and excited, as when you look forward to a relaxing vacation or an exciting date. For worry to exist, your thoughts about the future can't be hopeful or positive. They need to be *catastrophic*—the next key ingredient to worry. This is because when you worry, you think about the future in a highly negative light. Your thoughts focus almost exclusively on the worst possible outcomes and all the catastrophic implications of your future gone horribly wrong.

David, a Chicago entrepreneur, exemplified this catastrophic thought process. When he entered therapy, he had just started his first business, an Italian ice store. Opening this store in a trendy, upscale Chicago neighborhood had long been David's dream. He had spent much of his time at his previous job fantasizing about it. He always felt excited and hopeful when he pictured greeting his customers and serving them their favorite flavor on a hot summer day.

However, when the time came to open his doors for business, David felt incredibly anxious and worried. The joy and excitement he felt before was gone, replaced by fear and dread. Why the sudden shift? The reason is simple: David went from imagining all the joys of running his own business to focusing only on the catastrophic possibilities of the future. All day, his mind raced with negative thoughts along these lines: "What if I fail? I won't be able to get my old job back. My reputation will be ruined. No one will want to hire me. How will I pay my bills? Who will pay my son's college tuition? My wife will leave me. My son will resent me. I won't be able to provide for him. I'll lose my house. I'll end up penniless and broke. I'll be a laughingstock. My life will be over."

As you can see from David's dazzling display of worry, his thoughts meet both of our first two criteria of worry—he's focused on the future and he's thinking catastrophically.

The final key to our definition of worry was discovered by accident. Thomas Borkovec, a pioneer in worry research, originally set out to study insomnia. During his research with people who had trouble sleeping, he made an interesting breakthrough. He found that people who had difficulty sleeping suffered from excessive mental activity that seemed similar to worry. He also noted that this mental activity consisted largely of words, not images. His work with people suffering from insomnia led Borkovec to hypothesize that when people worry, they think almost exclusively in words (Borkovec 1979). Borkovec's subsequent research has confirmed this theory (Borkovec and Inz 1990).

This work is the basis of the final key to defining worry—that it consists largely of thoughts that are *language-based*. While in a normal, relaxed mood, we think in both words and images. However, while worry often starts with frightening images, those images are largely blocked out as words quickly move in and dominate your thinking. You can notice this for yourself the next time you worry by tuning in to your thoughts. What's going through your mind? You'll observe your inner voice taking over. Images—frightening or otherwise—get crowded out, as does the ability to think about anything else. Your thoughts are reduced to a one-track monologue forecasting a catastrophic future.

These three components, a focus on the future, catastrophic thinking, and verbal dominance, are the ingredients that make up worry. Borkovec and his colleagues concisely summarized these three components when they described worry as "talking to ourselves a lot about negative things . . . that we are afraid might happen in the future" (Borkovec, Ray, and Stöber 1998, 562). This description captures the true essence of worry.

TWO TYPES OF WORRY

Now that you understand what worry is, let's look at two different kinds of worry—*productive* and *unproductive*. Our patients often find it valuable to learn to distinguish between these two types of worry. Doing so allows them to acknowledge the important benefits of productive worry and set a more realistic goal of controlling unproductive worry. Understanding the difference between these two types of worry can be enormously helpful to you as well.

Productive Worry

It's important to understand that not all worry is bad. In fact, worry is an extremely important tool for our survival. As humans evolved, those who worried about their next meal—and took action to get more food as a result—survived and were more likely to thrive. Those who didn't were more likely to starve. In the same way, worry can help you solve problems and handle threats in your own life. For example, if you worry about your health, it might spur you to make some positive changes, such as quitting smoking or exercising more often. Those actions are the result of productive worry. Productive worry helps you solve real and immediate problems in your life—like paying an overdue credit card bill—or prompts you to reduce a realistic future threat, such as eating better to lessen the risk of heart disease. In short, productive worry is focused on a realistic problem and generates clear, specific steps to solve that problem.

UNPRODUCTIVE WORRY

Unproductive worry is the focus of the solutions described in this book. Two key components make worry unproductive. The first is that the worry generates no clear course of action. One of the biggest antidotes to anxiety and stress is taking productive action. Anxiety is your fight-or-flight response—your body's built-in mechanism for responding in the face of danger. It helps you to do something about the threat. Unfortunately, with unproductive worries that's impossible—these worries paralyze you, thwarting any effective action. Instead of taking specific steps to solve a real problem, you get stuck in the quagmire of unproductive worry.

The second thing that makes worry unproductive is a focus on an unlikely event, such as a plane crash or terrorism. Let's face it: life is risky. We face many dangers every day. However, by turning your attention to remote threats, you waste time and energy feeling needlessly tense and anxious. Worse yet, you might make decisions that diminish your quality of life based on these fears. For example, you might feel skittish about flying because you fear a plane crash. Certainly, planes can—and do—crash. However, statistically it's extremely rare. And by avoiding flying you miss out on the convenience and opportunities provided by air travel—all to prevent a disaster that's highly unlikely to happen. Contrast that with productive worry, which energizes you to make positive changes in your life, and you can see why unproductive worry is so destructive.

Exercise: Is Your Worry Productive?

The next time you catch yourself worrying, determine if it's productive or unproductive worry. You can do this by taking out your notebook and writing a clear description of your worry. For example, you might write, "I am going to fail my final exam." Once you've identified your specific concern, ask yourself the following questions:

- Am I focused on a realistic problem?
- Is the problem solvable?
- Is the worry motivating me to take action?
- Am I generating potential solutions?
- Am I acting on those solutions?

If you answered no to any of these questions, your worry is most likely unproductive, causing you unnecessary feelings of nervousness, anxiety, and stress.

The Impact of Worry

When you worry, it's a complete experience that affects the main parts of your emotional life—what you think, what you do, how you feel, and how you relate to others. To better understand worry's impact on you, let's take a look at each of these aspects: cognitive, behavioral, physiological, and interpersonal.

COGNITIVE

The cognitive aspect of worry consists of your thoughts when you feel worried. A "cognition" is simply a thought. As we noted in our definition of worry, negative, catastrophic thoughts about the future dominate your mind when you're worried. For example, people who worry about their health might have cognitions such as "What if I get cancer? I'll die a horrible, painful death. My family will suffer watching me waste away. It'll be awful. I couldn't stand it. The medical bills alone will bankrupt me. The chemo will make me so sick. What if I already have cancer? I might be sick and not even know it. This is terrible! I can't take it."

BEHAVIORAL

The behavioral component is how you react in response to worry. These responses usually fall into two general types. The first is an attempt to reduce your anxiety with some sort of action. This might mean seeking reassurance from a trusted friend, or you might resort to compulsive behaviors, such as checking or repeating.

The second behavioral component is avoidance. *Avoidance* simply means staying away from the sources of your anxiety or worry. This might take the form of procrastinating on a stressful task, dodging a friend you have a conflict with, or avoiding direct contact with your boss because you're worried she might fire you.

PHYSIOLOGICAL

Chronic worry is physically stressful and can cause a wide variety of bodily symptoms. Some of the more common symptoms that excessive worriers experience include muscle tension, difficulty concentrating, restlessness, fatigue, and insomnia (American Psychiatric Association 2000). In addition, you might notice other symptoms of anxiety, such as trembling, sweating, hot flashes, light-headedness, shortness of breath, nausea, diarrhea, or frequent urination.

INTERPERSONAL

Worry not only affects *you*, it also disrupts your relationships with other people. A recent survey by the Anxiety Disorders Association of America (ADAA) highlighted this problem (ADAA 2004). In their survey, they found that people who worry excessively are more likely to avoid social situations and intimacy with their partner. The survey also found that excessive worry leads to more frequent arguments and more missed days at work. While worry seems to negatively impact all types of relationships, the ADAA survey found that worry caused the greatest disruption in romantic relationships and friendships.

Here's a summary of the impact of worry on how you think, behave, feel, and relate to others:

- **Cognitive:** negative, catastrophic thoughts about the future

- **Behavioral:** avoidance, compulsive behaviors

- **Physiological:** muscle tension, insomnia, fatigue, restlessness, difficulty concentrating

- **Interpersonal:** avoidance of intimacy, arguing, irritability, withdrawal

Know Your Own Worry

Now that you have a clear definition of worry, you know the difference between productive and unproductive worry, and you understand the impact of worry on the major areas of your life, it's time for you to get to know *your* worry better. Of course, it might seem that you're already intimately familiar with your worry because if your worry is excessive and out of control, you might worry most of the time. However, we often find that our patients are overwhelmed and confused by the worry they experience and benefit greatly from a crash course in studying their worry. After all, the more you know about your enemy, the more likely you are to win the battle.

One way to familiarize yourself with your worry—and to regain control of it—is to closely monitor it. By simply tracking your worries, you can make an overwhelming problem more understandable and controllable. Below we'll show you how to monitor your worries so you'll know exactly what you worry about and when you worry about it. You'll gain more control over your worry as a result.

SELF-MONITORING

Tracking your worries by keeping a daily record of them is called *self-monitoring*. Self-monitoring is an effective technique with a long history in cognitive behavioral therapy. It's been successfully applied to problems as diverse as eating disorders (Allen and Craighead 1999) and compulsive hair pulling (Rapp et al. 1998). It's also a useful step in controlling worry.

One of the fascinating things about self-monitoring is how it changes your behavior. Remarkably, if you do too much of something, like biting your nails, simply monitoring the excessive behavior often reduces it. Along the same lines, if you do too little of something, like working out, tracking how often you exercise can result in more frequent trips to the gym. When self-monitoring is applied to chronic worry, the result is often less worry.

We've seen the dramatic effects of self-monitoring first-hand. One of our patients, an accountant named Nick, suffered from chronic, uncontrolled worry for several years. Most of the time, especially at work, Nick felt worried and tense. In the first session, he was instructed to track his worry over the next two weeks. He arrived at the next session with a big smile. He said he already felt much better and beamed, "I think you chased those worries away by asking me to track them!" For Nick, carefully monitoring his worries resulted in a much greater sense of control over them and a significant decrease in the amount of time he spent worrying.

Exercise: Monitor Your Worries

You can start tracking your own worries by recording them in your notebook. To do this, divide a sheet of paper into three columns. In the first column, record what you worried about. In the second, make note of when you worried, including the date and time. In the third column, record how anxious you felt on a scale of 1 to 10, with 10 being the most anxious.

Tips for Effective Self-Monitoring

Self-monitoring, like many of the strategies in this book, is simple but not easy. Here are some tips to make your efforts more effective:

- Keep your notebook handy so you can record your worry as it happens.

- Resist the urge to write it down later. Self-monitoring is most effective if it's completed immediately when worry strikes.

- Be as specific as you can when you describe your worries. Avoid vague descriptions like "I'm worried about everything" or "I just feel tense."

- Record all of your worries. Complete and accurate self-monitoring is critical to controlling worry for two reasons: You can't change something unless you're aware of it every time it happens. Plus, it's difficult to find themes and patterns in your worry if information is missing.

Common Themes of Worry

On the surface, there's a seemingly endless supply of things to worry about. However, as you monitor your own worries, you might discover something interesting that researchers studying worry have also found. It turns out that worry is not the bottomless pit it might seem. Instead, a surprisingly few number of common themes emerge. For instance, a study by Michelle Craske and her colleagues (1989) found that people tend to worry about these things the most:

- Family

- Health

- Finances

- Relationships

- Work or school

Do these sound familiar? As you track your own worries, you might find you worry about similar things. Admittedly, these categories are somewhat broad—under finances, for example, you could worry about your bills, the stock market, the value of your home, or your retirement—yet they also simplify your worry by making it smaller and easier to control. Identifying the topics you worry about most often is a key step in controlling worry.

Exercise: What Do You Worry About?

Now it's your turn to identify the topics of your worry. Below, we've listed common themes of worry. Review your self-monitoring record and check the ones you worried about over the past week:

- ❑ Finances
- ❑ Health (self)
- ❑ Health (others)
- ❑ Work or school
- ❑ Relationships
- ❑ Family
- ❑ Crime
- ❑ Safety
- ❑ Other

Find Your Core Worries

So far, you've used self-monitoring to learn what you worry about, when you worry, and which worries cause you the most anxiety. You can also use self-monitoring to provide you with one more piece of useful information: what you worry about the *most*. As you monitor your worries, you'll find that some worries pop up again and again. By identifying these worries and conquering them, you can defeat a big piece of your worry.

Exercise: What Are Your Core Worries?

After you've tracked your worries for at least a week, count how often you worried about each theme. What do you worry about most often? Is it your health? Your finances? Your relationships? Maybe it's your work or your family. Once you've identified your core worries, list them in your notebook.

A graduate student named Beth spent one week monitoring her worries using this technique. Each day, she recorded what she worried about, when she worried about it, and how anxious she felt while worrying. Through self-monitoring, she learned that she worried almost exclusively about three things: her finances, her health, and her relationship with her mother. Of these, worry about finances generated the most anxiety.

Beth also found that she worried primarily during quiet times, such as evenings and weekends. Other times, when she was busier and more distracted, she worried less and felt more in control of her worry. Using self-monitoring, Beth developed some control over her worry because she learned what she worried about, when she worried, and what worries caused the most anxiety. This information was highly valuable in therapy, as it helped Beth make actual changes and manage her worry more effectively. Gathering data in this way can also be useful to you as you work to manage your worry.

Key Points

- Worry consists of future-oriented, catastrophic thinking largely consisting of words, rather than images.

- Worry can be either productive or unproductive. Productive worry leads to direct action to solve a problem or reduce a future threat. Unproductive worry paralyzes you and inhibits problem solving.

- Worry affects how you think, behave, feel, and relate to others.

- Self-monitoring, in which you keep an accurate daily record of your worry, is an effective technique for helping control worry.

- To monitor your worry, keep track of what you worry about, when you worry about it, and how anxious you feel.

- People tend to worry about a few specific themes. These themes include finances, health, family, relationships, and safety. Use your self-monitoring records to determine the things you worry about most frequently. These fears are your core worries.

2

Make a Commitment

We'll start this chapter by asking you a question: Are you truly committed to learning to control your worry? Before you answer, though, it's important to understand what it takes to conquer worry. In this chapter, we'll give you the information you need to decide if you are committed to ridding your life of excessive worry. In the pages ahead, we'll describe the process of change and we'll help you identify the costs and benefits of excessive worry. Also, since worrying less has its own pluses and minuses, we'll discuss the pros and cons of learning to control worry. At the end of this chapter, you'll be asked again if you are ready to make a commitment to reducing your worry.

In some ways, making a commitment is the most important step you can take. Committing to change and sticking to that commitment is essential to your success. The methods in this book *do* work, but they need your consistent effort to be effective. That's why your commitment is so important.

How Change Works

As you consider making positive changes by reducing the amount of worry in your life, it's important to understand several key things about the process of learning to control worry. First, keep in mind that controlling worry is a skill and the learning process is similar to that for other skills you've mastered. For example, think about learning to drive a car. At first, it felt strange and overwhelming. You were suddenly in charge of controlling something you'd never had to control. It seemed impossible to remember everything. You had to hit the gas, put on your turn signal, look in the mirrors, shift gears, steer, and not crash—all at the same time! Like all new drivers, you made some mistakes. Maybe you accidentally ran a few stop signs or stalled at a red light. And who can forget that first traffic ticket? But after countless hours behind the wheel, driving has probably become second nature. Controlling worry is a lot like learning to drive. At first, the techniques will feel awkward and unusual. You may even feel somewhat overwhelmed. But, with consistent practice, managing worry will soon become second nature—just like driving.

It's also essential to know that learning to control your worry, like learning any other skill, takes time and effort. You'll get the most from the methods in this book if you set aside time on a regular basis to practice managing your worry. We see the benefits of consistent effort on a daily basis— among the patients in our practices, the ones who work persistently at controlling their worry invariably achieve the best results.

As you progress through the solutions described in this book, you'll discover that the road of personal growth is filled with peaks and valleys. If you work hard, you will inevitably make progress. However, you'll also have days when, despite your best efforts, it's hard to keep your worry in check. That's natural. You're learning a new skill, and you'll experience both successes and setbacks during the learning process. A patient of ours named Ellen is a good example of the ups and downs of learning to manage worry. Through persistence and hard work, she made tremendous progress in controlling her worry. In fact, she did so well that she wondered aloud at the end of therapy why she ever worried so much in the first place. As the dark clouds of worry faded from her life, they were replaced by sunnier, stress-free days.

However, worry inevitably reappeared on Ellen's horizon. Instead of viewing these expected challenges as setbacks—and feeling discouraged and defeated—Ellen chose to see them as golden opportunities to further refine her skills. By practicing her new skills in these challenging situations, she grew even more effective at handling worry. As a result, the times when she was filled with worry grew few and far between.

REALISTIC GOALS

Another key aspect of making successful changes in your life is setting realistic, attainable goals. Many of our patients come to therapy with the objective of eliminating worry from their lives. You might have that same goal in mind as you read this book. Like many of our patients, you too might define success as never worrying again. If you've suffered the ill effects of excessive worry, it's easy to understand why you'd feel that way.

Unfortunately, trying to completely eliminate worry is a self-defeating goal that sets you up for failure because it's unachievable. The truth is that some worry is a reality of life. It's when worry is persistent, out of control, and unproductive that it becomes a problem. That's why we stress setting the goal of controlling unproductive worry, not eliminating all worry.

Exercise: Setting Goals

What do you hope to accomplish as you read this book and complete the exercises? Perhaps you'd like to learn to control your worry about something specific, such as your children or your job. Or perhaps you want to learn strategies to control worry in general. You may also hope to master specific skills for managing worry, such as relaxation techniques or assertive communication. Think about the goals you want to achieve with this book and write them in your notebook.

REALISTIC EXPECTATIONS

Along with understanding the change process and setting clear, reasonable goals, it is also important to consider your expectations about change. Ask yourself how you expect to develop better control over your worry. You might plan to just read this book and feel better. Unfortunately, that probably won't work. Just like reading an exercise book won't get you in any better shape, merely reading this book without completing the exercises probably won't provide you with much relief.

Or, like some patients we see, maybe you believe that occasionally trying a few of the exercises in this book will do the trick. Unfortunately, this approach will most likely fail as well because excessive worry is a *chronic* problem. That means you've been this way for a while. As a result, it'll take some time and hard work to bring your worry under control. Change doesn't occur overnight. Mastering the skills necessary to manage your worry takes consistent practice and effort.

At times, it can be frustrating as you struggle with a particularly difficult worry. At other times, though, it's exhilarating.

Some of the happiest moments for our patients—and us—occur when they achieve victory over worry. That's when our patients say, with a big smile, "In the past, I would've really worried about that—but not now!"

The Costs and Benefits of Worry

Listing the costs and benefits of worry is a great place to start on your path to peace and happiness. By doing this first, you can make an informed decision about the need to control your worry.

Let's start with the costs of worry. Common costs of excessive worry include physical problems, irritability, relationship difficulties, an inability to relax and enjoy life, increased drug or alcohol use, and a lack of productivity. You may experience some or all of those consequences. You may also have some different costs. Think back over the last few months. What price have you paid for worrying too much?

Now let's look at the benefits. Believe it or not, worry actually has some advantages. People generally don't continue to do something unless it benefits them in some way. It's important to be fully aware of the rewards of your worry before you commit to change. Here are some common benefits of worry:

- **Distraction:** Your worry may divert your attention away from other things that bother you, such as an unhappy marriage or a job you dislike.

- **Reduction of anxiety:** Ironically, worry can *lower* your anxiety a bit by blocking out painful images and thoughts. Even though you still feel anxious when worrying, you don't feel the intense panic you might if you fully experienced the fearful scenarios that lurk in your imagination.

- **Superstition:** Many people who worry believe that worry protects them and prevents bad things from happening. If you hold this belief, you might fear that if you stop worrying, disaster will result. For instance, Bud, a fearful flyer, believed that if he didn't worry about his plane crashing, it would cause his flight to crash. To him, it felt as though his worry kept the plane in the air.

- **Attention and reassurance:** Your worried, anxious state can bring words of comfort from others. They console you and try to cheer you up when you're upset.

- **Avoidance of unpleasant events:** Your worry may get you out of things that you don't want to do. Instead of expressing yourself directly and assertively, you use your worry as an excuse to avoid things you find unpleasant.

- **Controlling others:** You may use your worry to control the behavior of other people. For example, if being away from your daughter upsets you, you may tell her you'll be worried sick if she travels in hopes that she will cancel her trip.

- **Preparation:** You may believe that by worrying excessively about some dreaded event now, you'll be prepared when it happens and it won't upset you. For example, Joan often worried her husband would leave her. Even though they had a good relationship, Joan felt that by worrying about divorce now, she wouldn't be devastated if her husband did ultimately decide to leave.

- **Problem solving:** You might believe that your worry actually helps you solve problems more effectively. It may feel as though, without worry, you wouldn't be able to handle the difficulties in your life.

The bad news is that if you start to worry less, you will lose these perceived advantages. The good news is that these changes aren't irreversible. In other words, if you want, you can always go back to worrying and reclaim these benefits. We are confident, though, that once you get a glimmer of life with control over your worry, you'll never go back.

Exercise: Conduct a Cost-Benefit Analysis

In your notebook, draw a line down the middle of a page. List the costs of your worry on one side and the benefits on the other side. List as many as you can. Now, look at each column and compare the two. Which side wins? Do the costs outweigh the benefits or vice versa? This will help you decide if worrying works more to your advantage or disadvantage.

The Pros and Cons of Learning to Control Worry

Let's assume, based on your cost-benefit analysis, you've decided that worrying has more costs than benefits and you want to learn to control your worry. How will learning to control your worry benefit you? In some ways, many of the benefits will simply be the opposite of the costs, such as feeling more relaxed or being less irritable around your family and friends. In addition, controlling your worry may bring many other benefits. These might include more confidence, increased productivity, fewer illnesses, a greater sense of peace and spirituality, and more joy and happiness.

Of course, there are also drawbacks to changing. Putting in time and effort to read this book and complete the exercises is one drawback. Some of the exercises, such as the relaxation techniques described in chapter 3, Learn to Relax, or the cognitive strategies listed in chapter 4, Change Your Thinking, involve a daily commitment of at least twenty to thirty minutes to achieve maximum benefit.

Another drawback is that some of the exercises, particularly in chapter 9, Confront Your Worries, and chapter 5, React Differently, may make you temporarily more anxious. Ultimately, of course, those strategies are designed to reduce your worry, but because they involve confronting something you fear, you may feel more distress initially while working on those solutions.

Exercise: Review the Pros and Cons

Now draw a line down the middle of a new sheet of paper in your notebook and list the pros and cons of learning to control your worry. Consider all possible benefits and drawbacks. Then review each column. Is it more to your advantage or disadvantage to learn to control your worry?

Commit to Change

At the beginning of this chapter, we asked you if you are committed to learning to control your worry. Now that you have a better understanding of how change works, along with more realistic expectations of what it takes to control worry, what do you think? As you analyzed the pros and cons, did you decide it's in your best interest to learn to manage worry? If so, it's time to finalize your commitment. Below is a contract that signifies your intention to work on controlling your worry.

Exercise: Sign a Contract

In your notebook, copy this contract and sign and date it: "I am making a commitment to work on controlling my worry. I understand that this will take time and effort. Because of this, I will set aside time regularly to work on the exercises in this book. I have decided that the costs of my worry outweigh the benefits, so I am committed to taking control of and reducing my worry." Be sure to review this contract, along with your lists of the costs of your worry and the benefits of learning to control it, whenever you feel your motivation waning a bit. It might also help to make your commitment public by sharing it with someone supportive in your life.

Key Points

- Persistence is the key in controlling worry. Change doesn't occur overnight; it's the result of consistent effort.

- Chronic, uncontrolled worry affects people in many ways. Know the personal costs and benefits of your worry. Before you commit to changing, be sure you've carefully considered the costs and benefits of your worry.

- Listing the pros and cons of mastering your worry can help you decide if such a change is truly in your best interest.

- Once you've decided to change, commit to investing the time and effort required for success. Make this commitment by signing a contract stating your intentions to work hard on your worry.

3

Learn to Relax

As many worriers know from experience, chronic uncontrolled worry can have troubling physical consequences. If left unchecked, worry can cause symptoms such as fatigue, headaches, muscle tension, trembling, irritability, sweating, hot flashes, light-headedness, shortness of breath, insomnia, nausea, diarrhea, and frequent urination.

These symptoms, seemingly unconnected, are the result of one thing: a nervous system that's in a constant state of arousal. In this chapter, we'll describe how the nervous system works and show you four relaxation techniques to counter chronic nervous system arousal. These techniques, practiced consistently, can change how you feel from tense and edgy to calm and stress free.

Your Two Nervous Systems

Before you embark on a regular relaxation program, it's important to understand how your nervous system works—or, more accurately, how your nervous *systems* work. You see, you actually have two nervous systems. Much like a car, your body has both an accelerator and a brake. The accelerator, known as the *sympathetic nervous system*, revs up during times of worry. When this happens, your body springs into action. Your heart beats faster, you breathe faster, your blood pressure rises, your mouth goes dry, and blood moves away from your digestive tract to your muscles. This is your fight-or-flight response in action. Evolution equipped us with this response to help us survive dangerous situations. Without it, it's unlikely humans would have survived very long.

On the other hand, the nervous system brake, known as the *parasympathetic nervous system*, slows your body down. When the parasympathetic nervous system is activated, your heart rate and respiration rate slow down, your blood pressure decreases, your muscles relax, and digestion takes place. You might notice the parasympathetic system at work the next time you feel very relaxed or as you drift off to sleep at night. Contrasting it with the fight-or-flight response, some call this the "rest-and-digest" response.

If you suffer from chronic worry, you have the gas pedal down most of the time. The brake—the parasympathetic system—doesn't get much use. Through practice, you've become very adept at speeding yourself up. But, along the way, your ability to slow down has gotten rusty. The techniques described in this chapter will help to restore this ability so you can once again unwind and relax.

Relaxation

In order to learn how to relax, you'll need specific relaxation techniques. In this chapter, you'll learn four different methods for achieving a deep state of relaxation:

1. Progressive muscle relaxation (PMR)

2. Diaphragmatic breathing

3. Guided imagery

4. Meditation

RELAXATION AS A SKILL

Before trying any of these approaches, it's important to understand that achieving a state of deep relaxation is a skill that takes practice. Thinking of relaxation as a skill might seem unusual. After all, relaxing isn't typically thought of as something you practice, it's just something you do. However, if you worry frequently, you probably find it difficult to relax. In fact, when you try to unwind, you may become frustrated because you still feel keyed up and on edge. Previously relaxing activities, such as gardening or reading, no longer create the feelings of peace and calm they once did. Instead, you feel worried and anxious almost all the time. Even falling asleep at night becomes difficult because it takes you longer and longer to relax and drift off to a peaceful sleep.

These changes occur because the ability to relax is a skill and chronic worry erodes that skill. However, with regular practice of the techniques described below, you'll learn to relax with ease once again.

BENEFITS OF REGULAR RELAXATION PRACTICE

Consistent relaxation practice has many proven benefits (Benson 1975), including the following:

- **Physical:** reduced heart rate, decreased respiration rate, lower blood pressure, reduced muscle tension, reduced oxygen consumption, increased energy

- **Cognitive:** enhanced concentration, sharper focus, improved memory

- **Emotional:** reduced general anxiety, less irritability, a more positive mood, a greater sense of well-being
- **Behavioral:** less substance use, improved sleep habits, increased productivity
- **Health:** fewer tension headaches, less pain, fewer gastrointestinal symptoms

CHOOSING A RELAXATION TECHNIQUE

If you experience a particularly troubling symptom as a result of your chronic worry, you can select the relaxation technique that specifically addresses your problem area. That way, you can fight fire with fire. For example, if you suffer from chronic muscle tension, which leads to headaches, neck pain, and lower back pain, you might start with progressive muscle relaxation since this technique specifically targets tense muscles.

For the same reason, if you tend to overbreathe and experience anxiety symptoms such as light-headedness, chest pain, or fatigue, diaphragmatic breathing might work better for you. The table below offers additional suggestions on selecting a relaxation technique. Consider this a rough guide. In reality, when you're fighting worry, any relaxation technique practiced regularly will be beneficial.

Relaxation Technique	Symptoms
Progressive muscle relaxation	Physical symptoms: muscle tension, tension headaches, neck aches, jaw pain, shoulder tightness, restlessness, insomnia
Diaphragmatic breathing	Respiratory symptoms: light-headedness, fatigue, chest pain or tightness, dizziness

Meditation	Cognitive symptoms: racing thoughts, what-if thoughts, ruminating, difficulty concentrating
Guided imagery	Mental images: scenes of catastrophe playing out in your mind (failing a test, your plane crashing, a presentation going poorly)

Specific Techniques

Below are descriptions of four relaxation techniques we use frequently in our practices. Each one, practiced regularly, is an effective method of achieving a deep state of relaxation.

PROGRESSIVE MUSCLE RELAXATION

In 1929, Edmund Jacobson described a method for achieving a deep state of calm in his book *Progressive Relaxation*. His technique, which he named progressive muscle relaxation (PMR), can help you achieve a deep state of physical relaxation by soothing the chronic muscle tension that keeps your sympathetic nervous system fired up. This technique was developed by Jacobson specifically to counter anxiety. He theorized that anxiety and relaxation are incompatible states. In other words, they can't occur at the same time. Thus, voluntarily achieving a relaxed state would defeat any anxiety a person experiences.

Before practicing PMR, take a moment to mentally scan your body. Where are you tense? In your jaw? Your neck? Your shoulders? Record the areas of tension you notice in your notebook and pay particular attention to these areas when you do PMR.

Instructions for PMR

The following instructions for PMR are based on Jacobson's technique. Each step describes a method to tense and relax specific muscles. Before you start PMR, be sure you are in a comfortable position and free from distractions. As you move through the steps of PMR described below, hold each tension position for ten seconds, and then relax as much as possible for twenty seconds before moving on to the next tension step. During each phase, attend to the feelings of tension and relaxation. Focus on the difference between these two states.

1. Lie on your back in a comfortable position.

2. Make a fist and curl your hands in toward your elbows, bending at the wrist and tensing your forearms. Pull your forearms toward your upper arms, flexing your biceps. Now release and let your hands, forearms, and upper arms relax. Focus on the difference between the sensations of tension and relaxation.

3. With your knees slightly bent, lift your legs up about six inches. Pull your toes upward toward your knees. Feel the tension in your calves and thighs. Now gently put your legs back down and relax your calf muscles and thighs. Notice the difference between the states of tension and relaxation.

4. Pull your stomach in toward your back, tightening your stomach muscles. Now release and relax your stomach muscles and focus on the difference in feeling between tension and relaxation.

5. Take a deep breath and as you inhale, feel the tension in your chest muscles and the muscles in

your rib cage. When you exhale, feel those muscles loosen and relax. Notice the difference between the feelings of tension and relaxation. Repeat twice.

6. Arch your back. Feel the tension in the muscles along your spine. Now gently lower yourself back down and relax your back completely. Feel the difference between tension and relaxation in your back muscles. (If you have a bad back, you might want to skip this step.)

7. Draw your shoulder blades backward, trying to get them to meet in the middle of your back. Now release them and relax completely, feeling the difference between tension and relaxation.

8. Shrug your shoulders up toward your ears and focus on the sensation of tension created in your shoulders and neck. Let your shoulders drop completely and focus on the relaxed feeling in your neck and shoulders.

9. Raise your eyebrows as high as possible, wrinkling your forehead. Notice the tension in the muscles in your forehead. Now relax those same muscles and focus on the feeling of relaxation.

10. Pull your eyebrows down as if you were frowning. Feel the tension in the muscles just above your eyes. Now relax those muscles and focus on that sensation.

11. Close your eyes tightly and feel the tension in the muscles around your eyes. Now release those muscles and relax completely.

12. Now just relax and release any remaining tension in your body. Focus on your breathing for a few minutes while taking deep, slow breaths.

PMR takes approximately twenty to thirty minutes to complete. Some find it helpful to record these instructions and then listen to the tape to guide them during PMR practice. If you make a tape, record the steps in a calm, soothing voice and allow ten seconds for each tension step and twenty seconds to relax between steps.

Following this routine once a day will help you develop an overall sense of calmness and reduce feelings of tension and worry. You may also experience fewer physical symptoms associated with worry, such as headaches and neck pain. Don't be concerned if you don't feel especially relaxed right away. Like any skill, PMR takes time to master. You may find it helpful to record your daily practices in your notebook, noting your overall level of relaxation, from 1 (very tense) to 10 (very relaxed), after each practice. This way you can track your progress as you develop this skill.

DIAPHRAGMATIC BREATHING

Chronic worry can alter your natural breathing patterns, resulting in poor breathing habits. The tension caused by worry often moves the location of your breath from your diaphragm—its natural source—up to your chest. This is known as *chest breathing*, and it tends to be shallow and rapid.

Humans weren't built to breathe into the chest. To see how we were built to breathe, watch a baby sleeping. The stomach gently expands and contracts in a slow, rhythmic way and the rib cage moves only a bit, if at all. Notice that the foundation of the breath is deep in the belly, focused mainly in the abdomen. This is known as *diaphragmatic breathing*.

Many people have lost the ability to breathe diaphragmatically over time. In fact, one of our colleagues claims that only trained singers breathe diaphragmatically as adults. Test your own breathing style by putting one hand on your chest and the other on your belly button. Take a few breaths. Which hand is moving? The more the hand on your chest moves, the more you are chest breathing.

Hyperventilation Syndrome

Chest breathing often results in hyperventilation. When you hear the term "hyperventilate," you may picture movie scenes where an actor dramatically huffs and puffs, and maybe even breathes into a paper bag. However, hyperventilation isn't always that exaggerated. In fact, it can be so subtle you may not even be aware it's happening. That's because hyperventilation is defined simply as taking in more oxygen than your body needs.

For example, if you're sitting at your desk working on your computer, the oxygen demands of your body are quite low. However, if you feel tense and worried, you may breathe slightly more rapidly than necessary, turning your breathing into a quick inhalation and an incomplete exhalation. When this occurs, the amount of oxygen you take in is more than the amount of carbon dioxide you exhale. As a result, the level of carbon dioxide in your blood decreases relative to the level of oxygen in your blood. This change, the result of hyperventilation, triggers an array of unpleasant physical symptoms, including these:

- Dry mouth
- Fatigue
- Light-headedness
- Shortness of breath
- Numbness and/or tingling
- Chest pains or tenderness
- Pounding, racing heartbeat

- Feeling anxious or tense
- Frequent sighing or yawning

Instructions for Diaphragmatic Breathing

Breathing diaphragmatically in a paced, controlled manner counteracts the unpleasant effects of hyperventilation and chest breathing. Here are the steps to diaphragmatic breathing:

1. Lie down in a comfortable position.

2. Scan your body for tension and relax any tense muscles.

3. Turn your attention to your breathing.

4. Place one hand on your chest and the other on your abdomen right above your belly button.

5. Breathe through your nose.

6. Try to move the location of your breath from your chest to your abdomen. Your chest should remain still. Your stomach should expand and contract easily, like a balloon, with each breath.

7. Slow your breathing down by counting to three as you inhale and to three as you exhale.

8. Continue for approximately ten minutes.

If you have trouble breathing with your abdomen, place a book on your stomach and practice moving it up and down with each breath. During practice, resist the urge to gasp, yawn, or overinhale. Instead, aim for smooth, fluid breaths. Once you slow your breathing down and use your diaphragm, your breathing will feel effortless and relaxed.

Once you've mastered this skill, you can use it easily and discreetly whenever you feel anxious. Simply place a hand on your abdomen and move your breath to your diaphragm. Then slow your breathing down by counting to three while you inhale and to three as you exhale.

GUIDED IMAGERY

When you feel anxious, your mind may flood with thoughts of disaster. You might predict catastrophes, such as losing your job or a raging fire engulfing your home. Adrenaline rushes through your veins, your pulse speeds up, and your breathing quickens. As a result, you feel anxious, worried, and tense.

Guided imagery counters those upsetting thoughts and images by using your mind's eye to calm you, not frighten you. Just as imagining disaster creates a state of anxiety, picturing a peaceful, relaxing scene instills a sense of calm, neutralizing the damaging effects of chronic worry.

Instructions for Guided Imagery

Your guided imagery practice shouldn't be rushed or interrupted, so you may need to plan in advance. Schedule about thirty minutes when you can focus on your practice, and select a quiet place where you won't be disturbed. When your scheduled time arrives, follow the steps below:

1. Lie down in a comfortable position.

2. Slow your breathing down.

3. Scan your body for tension and relax any tight muscles.

4. Continue breathing calmly and slowly as you vividly picture the imagery scene described below.

5. When you're finished, relax quietly for several minutes with your eyes closed.

To make your practice more effective, read the script below into a tape recorder in a calm, slow voice, allowing plenty of time to use your imagination. Then play the tape to direct your visualization during imagery practice.

Guided Imagery Scene

Picture yourself walking along a beach. The sun is shining high in a blue sky. It's warm and comfortable, and you feel the salty breezes cooling your skin. The water is a deep blue. Waves gently roll in. As you stroll, feeling the sand between your toes, you leave your worries far behind. You feel the warm sun on your skin and it calms you. Along the way, you come to a comfortable, quiet spot and choose to lie down.

You stretch out on a blanket and listen to the waves coming in to the shore. Your breathing starts to move with the rhythm of the waves. The sun, shining overhead, continues to warm your skin. You focus the warmth on your feet, feeling them becoming comfortably warm and heavy. Your breathing becomes deeper and slower, and the warmth of the sun spreads up your legs to your calves, then to your thighs and hips. Both of your legs are now pleasantly warm and heavy and relaxed. You notice the sounds of the waves gently rolling in and out, in and out, further soothing you.

Your breathing is deep and slow now, and you feel calm and relaxed. The gentle radiance of the sun now spreads from your legs up into your abdomen. You feel the muscles of your stomach relaxing with the warmth, becoming smooth, still, and relaxed. Your skin feels warm as your stomach rises up and down in time with the waves.

The warmth of the sun continues to spread throughout your body, moving up from your stomach and filling your chest. You feel a light glow in your chest, filling you with relaxation and peace. Your legs, stomach, and chest feel warm, heavy, and relaxed. You breathe with ease now, feeling only the warmth that is filling you.

Now the focus of the warmth moves to your fingertips and starts to relax them. That feeling moves through your hands, up into your forearms and biceps. Your arms get heavy, the muscles relaxing deeply as the warmth of the sun moves through them. Your breathing slows a little more as you sink even further into relaxation.

The relaxing warmth of the sun moves up into your shoulders and neck. You feel them ease and drop slightly as you allow yourself to relax under the warm sun. You notice how warm, heavy, and relaxed your muscles feel, from your toes to your shoulders, brought to a state of deep relaxation by the warm sun.

The relaxation moves throughout the rest of your body, up into your face. You feel these muscles loosen, your face becoming very smooth, open, and calm. The sun gently warms your face, soothing away any tension. You feel very peaceful now, as peaceful as you've ever felt. You are deeply relaxed.

Breathe easily now and just enjoy the feeling of deep relaxation. Notice how warm and heavy you feel, how perfectly calm and relaxed you are at this moment. Bask in the sun, feeling the golden rays covering your skin, bringing soothing warmth to you, making you feel completely calm. You are fully relaxed.

Many other guided imagery scripts are available. For more information on guided imagery and additional scripts, see Martin Rossman's *Guided Imagery for Self-Healing: An Essential Resource for Anyone Seeking Wellness* (2001) or Julie T. Lusk's *30 Scripts for Relaxation, Imagery and Inner Healing* (1993). You also can purchase audiotapes or CDs with a variety of guided imagery scripts at most bookstores.

MEDITATION

Meditation dates back to the very beginning of recorded history, and perhaps even further, which gives you a sense of how long people have sought inner peace and relaxation. Originally a spiritual practice, meditation evolved over the centuries into a relaxation technique practiced around the world.

The main goal in meditation is a calm mind and a heightened awareness of the present. This is in direct contrast to the typical mental state of the chronic worrier, whose mind is often overly active and filled with fears about the future. Calming your mind and focusing on the present will allow your body to release unnecessary tension and relax. This results in an increased sense of inner calm and decreased feelings of nervousness and anxiety.

Instructions for Meditation Practice

There are many different meditation techniques from which to choose. Edmund Bourne, author of *The Anxiety and Phobia Workbook* (2005), offers these straightforward and effective guidelines for meditation:

1. Find a quiet place where you won't be disturbed.

2. Sit in a comfortable position.

3. Choose a neutral word to focus on, such as "one" or "tree." This word is your mantra.

4. Focus on your breathing.

5. Silently repeat your mantra once upon each exhalation.

6. When other thoughts come into your mind, simply let them pass through and return your focus to your mantra.

7. Continue for approximately ten to twenty minutes.

Remember to maintain a passive attitude during meditation. Simply permit relaxation to occur naturally. As with all relaxation techniques, regular practice is essential to achieve the full benefits meditation has to offer. Aim to practice once or twice per day.

Key Points

- Your nervous system is comprised of an accelerator (the sympathetic system) and a brake (the parasympathetic system). If you worry a lot, your foot is usually on the gas pedal, causing a variety of unpleasant symptoms.

- Relaxation techniques, such as PMR, diaphragmatic breathing, guided imagery, and meditation, activate your body's brake, slowing down your nervous system and countering the effects of chronic stress.

- Remember, relaxation is a skill. Consistent practice improves your ability to calm yourself and ward off anxiety. For maximum benefit, devote twenty to thirty minutes each day to practicing these techniques.

- Experiment with different techniques to find out what works best for you. Also, try matching the technique to a symptom you experience.

- During relaxation practice, maintain a passive attitude. The harder you try to relax, the less relaxed you will become in the process.

4

Change Your Thinking

In the last chapter, you learned specific techniques to counter the physical arousal that occurs when you feel anxious. This chapter focuses on the role of your thinking in making you feel anxious and stressed. We'll show you the connection between your thoughts and your feelings and describe the role of distortion in your thinking. We'll also teach you specific strategies to challenge and modify your thoughts.

A Brief History of Cognitive Therapy

In the 1960s, psychiatrist Aaron T. Beck and psychologist Albert Ellis, working separately, created a new model of treatment to relieve psychological distress. Fueled by dissatisfaction with the psychoanalytic school of thought, where problems are viewed as the result of unconscious issues, they sought a new way of looking at and treating mental illness.

As they worked on their new theories, they made two revolutionary discoveries. First, they found the source of our distress isn't unconscious at all. Through both clinical observation and rigorous research, Beck and Ellis, along with other cognitive theorists such as Donald Meichenbaum, discovered that your own *thoughts* determine how you feel, not internal conflicts operating outside your awareness. Beck called this theory that thoughts determine emotions the "cognitive model."

As Beck developed his theory, he made a second crucial discovery. He found that those who suffer emotional distress often also engage in distorted thinking. In other words, negative feelings, such as anxiety or depression, often result from faulty interpretations of the world. For example, a person feeling anxious at a crowded party may think that everyone is judging and critiquing her, despite a lack of evidence. In fact, she may even take positive cues, such as smiling or laughter, as evidence that others are making fun of her. As a result, she feels worried and tense and withdraws from the crowd. However, as you can see from this example, it's not the situation that's making her anxious. It's her distorted thinking.

Based on this new theory of emotional distress, Beck developed innovative therapeutic interventions to test these ideas in clinical practice. In applying these therapeutic techniques, he found that correcting these distortions and substituting more rational and realistic thoughts dramatically changed how people felt. This helped confirm his notion that distorted thinking is at the root of bad moods. Many subsequent researchers studying the effectiveness of this type of therapy on a variety of problems, including depression, panic attacks, and worry, have further validated Beck's theory.

Beck's therapy, aimed at correcting distorted thoughts and beliefs, is known as *cognitive therapy*. His writings (Beck et al. 1979; Beck, Emery, and Greenberg 1985), along with those of other cognitive therapists such as David Burns (1999b), Albert Ellis (Ellis and Harper 1975), and Robert Leahy (2003), form the basis for the theory and strategies presented in this chapter.

Exercise: Picture a Lemon

You can conduct your own experiment to test the impact of your thoughts by completing the following exercise: Close your eyes and imagine a bright yellow lemon sliced in half on a clean white plate. You see the juice from the lemon running onto the plate and you smell the fresh, citrus scent. Now imagine that you pick up half of the lemon, squeeze it gently, and then take a bite into it. You taste the lemon juice and feel it on your tongue as your taste buds react to the sour flavor. Now, notice what's happening to you physically. Is your mouth filled with saliva? This is your body reacting to a vivid mental image—a cognition. In fact, in many cases, your body reacts as if what you imagine is actually happening.

Cognitions and Worry

As you saw in the exercise above, your thoughts powerfully impact how you feel. And, just as your thoughts made your mouth water without food, they can also make you feel stressed and anxious in the absence of real danger. In other words, when you imagine a catastrophe, like having a heart attack or losing someone you love, you feel anxious. These thoughts and images make your muscles clench, your heart race, and your palms sweat. Remember, though, that you feel the way you think, so if you feel anxious, there's a good chance you're thinking anxious thoughts. These thoughts play a key role in your anxiety. Without these frightening thoughts, images, or daydreams, it's virtually impossible to experience the anxious apprehension associated with frequent worry.

Your anxious thoughts, and how they make you feel, are like a horror movie. Think back to a scary movie you once watched. Maybe it was *Jaws* or *Psycho*. Did you jump when a door slammed? Did you scream when the villain jumped out from a closet? Did your muscles tense as the suspense heightened? Of course, none of the terror in the movie was actually happening to you, but your body reacted as if you were the one in danger. As you can see from your reactions, your body often doesn't distinguish between what is real and what is imagined. The same thing happens when you play scary movies in your mind in the form of worries: You react as if your fears are actually occurring. The result is anxiety. As you learn to control worry, one of your main tasks is to identify the horror movies—in the form of catastrophic thoughts—playing in your mind.

Exercise: Identify Your Anxious Thoughts

To practice identifying your anxious cognitions, reflect back on a time during the past week when you felt worried or tense. What went through your mind? What scenes played in your imagination? What catastrophes did you predict? Write down your thoughts in your notebook. Be as specific and as complete as you can.

Common Cognitive Distortions

As stated earlier, cognitive therapy assumes when people feel anxious in the absence of an immediate threat, they are making faulty inferences about themselves, others, and the world.

Cognitive therapists call these faulty inferences *cognitive distortions*. These distortions typically take on a few specific forms. The sections below describe cognitive distortions that occur frequently in worry. Read them carefully and consider your own thoughts. Do any of these sound familiar? Do you see any of these distortions in your thinking when you worry?

OVERESTIMATING THE THREAT

Those who worry often *overestimate*, or exaggerate, the likelihood of a negative outcome. In this distortion, a remote, improbable negative event feels very likely. In other words, the possibility of a catastrophe is confused with its probability. Almost anything is possible, but many things that people worry about, such as dying of a rare illness or getting completely rejected by everyone, simply aren't probable.

Here are some examples of overestimating the threat. Note that in each case the catastrophic event *is* possible. Then ask yourself, even if these events are possible, *how likely* are they?

- Fearing standard childhood vaccinations, despite an extremely low incidence of complications

- Thinking adequately cooked beef may cause diseases like mad cow or E coli

- Assuming you'll get fired from your job if you're a few minutes late

- Worrying that you'll get trapped in an elevator and starve to death

MIND READING

As you might imagine, *mind reading* commonly occurs in those worried about social situations. As the name suggests, this distortion consists of guessing what others are thinking. In most cases, mind reading is the assumption that other people are thinking negatively about you. Usually, there's little or no evidence to support this assumption. Here are a few examples of mind reading:

- If I do poorly on this presentation, my coworkers will think I'm stupid.
- Other people are constantly critiquing me and my performance.
- Everyone thinks I'm ugly.
- People would think I'm a weirdo if they really knew me.

ALL-OR-NOTHING THINKING

All-or-nothing thinking, or black-and-white thinking, means viewing things in extreme categories. For example, you might describe a presentation you gave as "perfect" or "horrible." Instead of a more balanced, reasoned view, you overlook the shades of gray, the subtleties of life, and force experiences into either-or categories. Here are a few examples of all-or-nothing thinking:

- Believing that flying is "dangerous"
- Describing yourself as "irresponsible" if you overlook a task
- Labeling the job market as "bad" when you are looking for work
- Calling yourself a "failure" if you don't meet an important personal goal

CATASTROPHIC THINKING

Catastrophic thinking means describing unpleasant experiences in highly exaggerated terms. Albert Ellis (Ellis and

Harper 1975) called this *awfulizing*. Here, you see the feared scenario as horrible, awful, or unbearable. You tell yourself you couldn't stand it if the worst happened.

Even events that are actually negative can be subjected to catastrophic thinking. For example, one man who worried about becoming ill claimed that people with a terminal illness such as cancer "live in constant terror." In reality, of course, it's natural to feel fear in that situation, but people with fatal diseases usually learn to adapt and don't live in constant terror. Here are a few examples of catastrophic thoughts:

- It would be awful if someone noticed I was sweating.

- If I lost my job, my life would be over.

- I couldn't handle it if I got sick.

- I can't stand being stuck in traffic.

"SHOULD" STATEMENTS

"Should" statements make people feel pressured, rushed, and stressed. They create an unnecessary sense of urgency and foster the illusion that disaster awaits if you don't comply with the "should." "Should" statements directed at yourself are often a key source of guilt feelings. Those directed toward other people typically generate feelings of anger.

There's also often a hidden message in these types of cognitions: If you don't follow these rules, you are a failure. Albert Ellis built much of his therapy, known as rational-emotive behavior therapy, around eliminating "should" thoughts. Here are a few examples of "should" statements:

- I should exercise five times a week.

- I should keep a perfectly clean house.

- I should never get angry.

- I should get straight A's.

WHAT-IF THINKING

What-if thinking is a double-edged sword. On one hand, it can inspire creativity, invention, and discovery. Asking "What if we could land a man on the moon?" made a miracle happen. However, this question can also create misery, such as when you ask yourself, "What if something really bad happens?" Then, instead of exploring wonderful possibilities, what-if thoughts generate endless examples of feared disasters. Here are a few examples of what-if thinking:

- What if my daughter gets killed in a car accident?

- What if I left the stove on at home and my house burns down?

- What if I have a panic attack and embarrass myself?

- What if I did my taxes wrong and get arrested?

MENTAL FILTERING

Mental filtering means picking a negative aspect of a situation and dwelling on it. In reality, every circumstance is a complex mix of both positives and negatives. Ruminating only on the negatives sours your mood. In addition, by selectively focusing on the negatives, you filter out other, more positive information.

A variation of mental filtering occurs when you think only of the risks in a situation and ignore the benefits. For example, if you are facing surgery, you might focus only on the risks of the procedure and ignore the potential benefits to your health. Here are a few examples of mental filtering:

- Refusing to ride a train because of a recent accident

- Ruminating about the one person who fell asleep during your presentation while overlooking that others showed interest

- Focusing on the ruined dessert in a meal you prepared and disregarding how well the other dishes came out

- Remembering only the instances when your spouse was late and overlooking the times when she was punctual

OVERGENERALIZATION

Overgeneralization means making broad, global inferences based on a few limited events. Key watchwords for this type of thinking include overly inclusive terms such as "always" and "never." Here are a few examples of overgeneralization:

- Assuming you'll never get a job because you received one rejection letter

- Believing that you'll never find a partner after one person turns you down for a date

- Thinking that you'll always suffer from anxiety because of a particularly worry-filled day

- Telling yourself "I'm never on time" when you run late for an important meeting

DISCOUNTING COPING SKILLS

Anxious people not only often perceive danger when none exists, they also overlook positives that do exist, including their ability to cope with problems. If you tune in to your thinking the next time you catch yourself worrying, you'll probably notice that you exaggerate the threat and minimize your ability to cope with that threat. This double whammy leads to feelings of anxiety. Here are some examples of this type of thinking:

- I can't handle it.
- I wouldn't be able to stand it.
- Nothing would help.
- I can't do anything to manage this problem.
- I'm helpless.

Exercise: Identify Your Cognitive Distortions

Look back at what you wrote for the exercise earlier in this chapter where you identified your anxious thoughts during a particular incident when you felt worried. Use the checklist below to identify the cognitive distortions in your thinking. Check each one that applies.

◻ Overestimating the threat

◻ Mind reading

◻ All-or-nothing thinking

◻ Catastrophic thinking

◻ "Should" statements

◻ What-if thinking

◻ Mental filtering

◻ Overgeneralization

◻ Discounting coping skills

Remember, identifying your anxious thoughts and cognitive distortions is a key step in controlling your worry. The next time you feel anxious, listen to what's going through your mind. Chances are that thoughts and images of future catastrophe are running rampant. These thoughts and images play a large role in creating and maintaining your anxiety.

The solution is modifying your cognitions by using more realistic ideas to challenge your thinking. By substituting more realistic and rational thoughts for your unrealistic, distorted ones, you *can* change the way you feel!

Specific Techniques to Change Your Thinking

Gaining control over your worries requires specific methods to challenge and change your anxiety-producing thoughts. This means thinking more realistically about the future, including more accurately assessing the probability of a negative event and reevaluating your view of the impact of such an event. And since most people who worry greatly minimize their coping skills, you may need to develop a more realistic sense of your ability to handle challenges.

You've already identified some of the thoughts that cause you anxiety and have found the cognitive distortions in those thoughts. Now use the techniques listed below to challenge your thoughts and replace them with more reasonable, rational cognitions.

COUNTER CATASTROPHIC THINKING

When you're anxious, your mind fills with catastrophic thoughts and images. One antidote is to ask yourself a series of questions designed to "decatastrophize" your thinking. Here are some examples to help you counter your catastrophic thinking:

- What is the worst-case scenario?
- How likely is the worst-case scenario?
- What could I do to cope if the worst did happen?
- What are at least three other possible outcomes?
- What is the most likely outcome?
- How often have I been right in the past when I've predicted disaster?

Exercise: Challenge Your Catastrophic Thinking

Identify at least one catastrophic thought each day and write it down in your notebook. Record the level of anxiety associated with this thought on a scale of 1 to 10. Ask yourself the questions above, writing down your answers below your catastrophic thought. Rate your anxiety again after answering the questions above.

Here's an example: Mary is a stockbroker who often worried about losing her job. Here's how Mary challenged this catastrophic thought:

Negative Thought: *I will lose my job.*

Anxiety Level: 8

What is the worst-case scenario?
I could become homeless.

How likely is the worst-case scenario to occur?
Probably not very.

What could I do to cope if the worst did happen?
I could go live with my sister.

What are at least three other possible outcomes to the worst-case scenario?
1. I would find another job.
2. I could live off my savings.
3. I could go back to school and start a new career.

What is the most likely outcome?
If I do get fired, I'll survive and find another job.

How often have I been right in the past when I've predicted disaster?
Never.

Revised Anxiety Level: 2

EXAMINE THE EVIDENCE

When people feel anxious, they tend to treat their thoughts as though they're true without considering the facts. Examining the evidence encourages healthy skepticism about your thinking. In other words, anxious thoughts can and should be subjected to the same scrutiny as our other thoughts. They don't deserve to be treated as fact without solid evidence to back them up. Use the following questions to test out your worry thoughts and see if they really are true:

- What specifically am I predicting will happen?

- What are the facts about my prediction?

- What is the evidence for this prediction?

- What is the evidence against this prediction?

- Which side is more convincing?

- Based on the available evidence, what would I suggest a friend do in the same situation?

- What can I do about this now?

Use the above questions to challenge your negative predictions. People who worry often assume the worst based on little or no data. Sticking to the facts helps control this tendency.

For example, Joan convinced herself that she was going to fail an important exam. However, after examining the evidence she saw that she studied hard, did well on previous exams, always attended the class, and met with the professor to help her clear up any areas of difficulty. This evidence called into question her assumption that she was destined to fail, and she felt much less worried. She also followed the suggestions she gives friends when they worry about tests: Relax, make sure you know the material, get a good night of sleep, and go do well!

COST-BENEFIT ANALYSIS

Despite all the misery worry brings, it actually serves an important function at times. The benefit of controlled worry is that it can help you solve problems. However, as you know, worry run amok is unproductive. Use the questions below to put worry under the microscope so you can decide if it's actually benefiting you:

- How will worrying about this help me?

- What are the drawbacks of worrying about this?

- Based on this evaluation, is worrying about this helpful or harmful to me?

Exercise: Do a Cost-Benefit Analysis

Divide a sheet of paper down the middle. On the left side, list the costs of worrying about a specific issue. On the right, list the benefits. Assign points to each side based on how significant or important the costs and benefits are to you. Make sure the total number of points for both sides adds up to 100. Remember to list such consequences as physical problems, sleep difficulties, and relationship issues. Once you assign the points to each side, which side wins? Do the costs outweigh the benefits or vice versa?

Edward, a forty-year-old accountant, frequently worried about being late. Edward believed he, and others, should always be on time. Here's Edward's cost-benefit analysis of the belief "I should always be on time."

Costs	Benefits
I feel rushed, pressured, and stressed.	*I'm usually on time.*
I drive like a maniac.	*My coworkers see me as punctual.*
I get tension headaches.	
I snap at my coworkers, spouse, and children.	
I overreact to things like traffic.	
I panic if I run late.	
I get angry when others run late.	
Score	
85	*15*

This exercise showed Edward that his worry about being late hurt him more than it helped. He also realized he could still strive to be on time without panicking if he ran late. This realization liberated Edward from this particular worry, allowing him the freedom to accept inevitable inconveniences without undue stress.

TIME MACHINE

Robert Leahy described the time machine strategy in his book *Cognitive Therapy Techniques* (2003). The gist of it is that if you worry about a specific event, like losing a loved one or getting fired, you are probably focused on the immediate consequences of that event and overlooking how things change as time passes. The old adage "Time heals all wounds," or, as one of our patients said, "Time scars over all wounds," contains a good deal of truth. You can see this for yourself by thinking back to a challenge or setback you faced, such as an illness or a financial problem. In looking at that situation, you'll see that the most challenging part occurred first. As time went on, you coped with the problem more effectively. That's the key to the time machine technique. Using the questions below, you can peer into the future and see how your feared catastrophe affects you as time goes by:

- If my feared outcome occurs, how will I feel about it one month from now? How will I feel six months from now? One year? Five years? Ten years?

- What would I be doing to cope with this problem one month from now? Six months? One year? Five years? Ten years?

Exercise: A Ride in a Time Machine

Select a worst-case scenario that worries you, such as losing your job or your spouse. On a piece of paper, write a detailed description of your response to this event at the time frames in the questions above. How would you feel? What would you be doing? How would you be coping? What would change over time?

For example, Kathryn often worried about her parents dying. As is typical of worry, she only focused on the immediate pain of such a loss if it did occur. She thought about how awful it would feel and how much she would miss them. Using the time machine technique to reevaluate her view of the situation, she considered how she might feel and cope as time passed. Through that process, she saw the loss of her parents in a less catastrophic, more realistic way. Rather than viewing this loss as an unbearable hardship, she saw it instead as very difficult, especially in the beginning, but something she could gradually cope with as time went on.

STAY IN THE PRESENT

Worry can serve an ironic purpose. By creating horrific scenarios of the future, worry can serve as a distraction from problems in the present that are more mundane but real. By refocusing on your actual problems in the present, you can develop practical solutions and reduce the negative consequences of worry. Here are some key questions to ask yourself when you're worrying:

- What's *really* bothering me?

- Are there any specific problems that I am dealing with right now?

- What can I do today to make things better?

- What actions can I take to solve my current problems?

Exercise: Coping in the Present

The next time you catch yourself worrying, review these questions. They will help you stay in the present and reduce worry. Focusing on what's actually happening instead of what might happen is a crucial step in decreasing your anxiety. Listing steps for dealing with your problems and acting on them also leads to constructive action, a powerful antidote to worry.

Sheila used worry as a distraction whenever real-life problems popped up. As soon as she faced a challenge, her old worries about the health and safety of her children popped back up like a jack-in-the-box. Over time, she learned to use these worries as a cue that she needed to address an important *real* problem. By asking herself the questions above, she uncovered her hidden problems and developed strategies to deal with them directly instead of using worry to cover up what really bothered her.

Key Points

- In this chapter, you learned about the role your thinking plays in how you feel. In essence, if you feel anxious, chances are you are thinking negative, worrisome thoughts.

- Identify your anxious thoughts by writing them down on paper.

- Review the list of cognitive distortions and identify the distortions in your thoughts.

- Use the cognitive methods to clear up your cognitive distortions and substitute more realistic and rational responses for your worry thoughts.

- Practice, practice, practice! Keep working until you change your thoughts and reduce your worry.

5

React
Differently

Diane is an outgoing twenty-eight-year-old who sought therapy for worry. At the time of treatment, she was a full-time student with a two-year-old son, struggling to make ends meet using student loans and a small savings account. Not surprisingly, Diane worried about money. And whenever she worried about money, she reacted the same way—she scoured her budget over and over, trying in vain to wring extra money out of it.

Julie is a bright, hardworking thirty-four-year-old physical therapist. She has an eight-year-old son whom she loves deeply. While in therapy for worry, Julie tearfully described her main fear. She said, "I'm worried sick that my son will die in his sleep. I'm terrified that I'll go to wake him up in the morning and he'll be dead." As you might imagine, this worry made sleep almost impossible for Julie. Night after night, she tossed and turned, her mind flooded with thoughts of her son dying in his bed. As Julie spoke of the tight grip this fear had on her, she explained how she responded to it. She told her therapist, "Whenever I'm worried about my son dying, I check on him to make sure he's still alive. Just seeing him breathe helps me relax for a few minutes."

Diane's and Julie's reactions to worry, scouring the budget and checking on a sleeping child, are known as *worry behaviors* (Brown, O'Leary, and Barlow 2001). This chapter focuses on these behaviors—how you react after worry strikes. As you'll see, this reaction has a powerful impact on your worry. You'll also learn how changing this response can bring your worry under control.

What Are Worry Behaviors?

Worry behaviors are actions taken in response to worry that reduce your anxiety. What sets worry behaviors apart from real problem solving is that worry behaviors don't have any true impact on the outcome of events. The key to telling the difference lies in the purpose of the behavior. Does it actually address the problem you face, or does it just make you *feel* better? Diane coped with her worry by repeatedly balancing her budget. Julie dealt with her fear by checking on her son. These behaviors temporarily lessened each woman's anxiety but didn't change the end result. Diane didn't suddenly have more money after balancing her budget repeatedly, and Julie's son didn't survive the night because of his mom's constant checking.

An old joke captures the essence of these maladaptive responses to worry. It goes like this: A man visits a village and is awoken at sunrise by the sound of a loud trumpet. He gets out of bed, walks across the village, and finds the trumpet player.

"Excuse me, but what are you doing?" the sleepy visitor asks.

The trumpet player eagerly responds, "Keeping the elephants away from the village, Sir!"

A bit perplexed, the visitor politely points out that there are no elephants anywhere near the village.

The man with the trumpet smiles proudly and responds, "Exactly, Sir!"

In this joke, the worry behavior is playing the trumpet. Of course, the music has no impact on elephants trampling the village. But by playing music each morning, the trumpet player feels less anxious about the possibility of an elephant stampede. Such is the nature of worry behaviors. They don't really do anything, but it feels like they do.

HOW WORRY BEHAVIORS WORK

You might wonder why someone would continue these behaviors—why Diane crunches her budget or why Julie repeatedly checks her son—when they don't actually influence the outcome of events. There are several reasons. The first reason is that worry behaviors cause a temporary reduction in anxiety. In other words, after completing these behaviors, you feel less anxious. The problem, however, is that worry inevitably returns. And when that happens, you'll feel compelled to perform the worry behavior all over again. The result is a vicious cycle. Because these behaviors neither solve the problem nor eliminate your worry, you must repeat them each time worry strikes.

Worry behaviors also convince you that your actions prevent disaster. It's a compelling argument. Take the case of Julie. Several times a night, she checks on her son. And each morning he wakes up full of smiles and ready for breakfast. The end result is that Julie concludes it's her checking that's kept him safe. But why is he really still alive? Is it her checking? Or is it that her fear—her son dying in his sleep—is extremely unlikely?

Another reason you might continue these worry behaviors is your perception of the consequences if you *don't*. For instance, imagine that you are a cave dweller living in prehistoric times. Ever since you can remember, there's been a nightly routine of dinner followed by chanting in a circle. As you grew older, you found out that the chant is to ensure that the sun will rise the next day. Certainly, the sun rising is critical. If it doesn't, the result would be catastrophic. And the chant seems to work. Each night you chant, and sure enough the sun rises the next day. One day, it's your turn to lead the chant. Do you want to be the one to call it off? What if the sun doesn't rise the next day? Would you want that on your shoulders? It's that fear of the consequences of eliminating worry behaviors that bullies you into performing them each time you worry.

COMMON TYPES OF WORRY BEHAVIORS

After years in clinical practice, we're convinced that there's an endless variety of worry behaviors. However, the different worry behaviors we see usually fall into a few specific categories, the most common being superstition, checking, repeating, excessive preparation, excessive conscientiousness, reassurance-seeking, and avoidance.

Superstitions: These worry behaviors are attempts to reduce or prevent your feared outcome from happening. By performing these behaviors, you convince yourself that you've decreased or eliminated the risk you faced. Practically speaking, however, these behaviors have no real impact on the likelihood that what you worry about will actually occur. For example, Sarah is a thirty-year-old administrative assistant who travels frequently for work. Whenever Sarah travels, she refuses to wear black and she never books a hotel room on the thirteenth floor. Sarah believes that both of these behaviors reduce her chances of dying while traveling. As is the essence of worry behavior, these actions make Sarah feel better, but they have no effect on her actual safety.

Checking: As the name suggests, this type of worry behavior involves repeatedly checking to lessen your anxiety. Geoff, a thirty-seven-year-old accountant with two young children, relies on checking as his worry behavior whenever his fear of carbon monoxide poisoning strikes. He copes with this fear by checking the carbon monoxide detectors in his home several times a day to make sure they work.

Repeating: This is doing something over and over in response to a worry. It might mean reiterating something you said numerous times or repeating an action several times. For example, Dan, an experienced trial lawyer, worries about accidentally misleading someone during a conversation. He fears giving the wrong information, such as bad directions or an incorrect phone number. Dan deals with this worry by repeating himself excessively during conversations to ensure the person he's talking to is not misled.

Excessive preparation: A good example of this worry behavior comes from Doug, a college professor who suffers from chronic worry. One of Doug's greatest fears is being unprepared for his lectures. He worries that a student will ask a question that he's unable to answer. In his mind, if that happened, all of the students in his class would think that he's incompetent and word of his gross ineptitude would spread like wildfire to the faculty, culminating in a humiliating public firing. Doug copes with this worry by preparing excessively for class. Each day he prepares for several hours for his weekly lecture. This overpreparation culminates on the day of his class, when he spends eight hours getting ready for a one-hour lecture! Other examples of overpreparation include cleaning your home extensively before guests visit, studying excessively before an exam, and carrying a pharmacy of over-the-counter medications with you just in case you get sick.

Excessive conscientiousness: This worry behavior consists of taking extreme measures to avoid offending other people or violating a moral code. Consider Sophie, a mother of four. One of her main worries is offending other people by doing something "wrong" or "unethical." In response to this fear, Sophie takes the positive ideals of morals and ethics to the extreme. In therapy, she told of the time she drove an hour out of her way to repay a friend who had given her some spare change to make a small purchase. You may notice similar behavior in yourself if you share the worry that other people might look down on you or think less of you if you don't do what is "right" at all times.

Reassurance-seeking: The essence of reassurance-seeking is trying to eliminate doubt. You might ask for reassurance from friends or family members. You might consult experts, like doctors, for reassurance. Or you might compulsively search the Internet, books, or other sources of information. However you go about it, the goal is to find a guarantee that your fear won't come true. For example, Keith, a successful financial analyst, worried constantly about his health. Each time he felt a new pain or a weird twinge, he got on the Internet and sought reassurance that he was healthy. Sometimes he felt convinced, after hours of searching, that it was nothing. Other times, he still felt anxious and would rush to the doctor for a series of tests to reassure himself. Unfortunately, the comfort of receiving a clean bill of health was always short-lived. When a new pain appeared, Keith began his search for certainty all over again.

Avoidance: Avoidance is a key feature of chronic anxiety and worry. The belief behind avoidance is that if you stay away from your fears, they won't come true. For example, one of our patients, Ben, is an active forty-year-old professional. One of his biggest goals in life is getting married and having a family. Unfortunately, one of his greatest fears is that he'll get stuck in an unhappy marriage. The result of this fear is that Ben avoids dating as much as possible. And when he does date, he quickly finds something wrong with the woman he's seeing and ends the relationship before it gets more intimate. In this way, Ben avoids the risk of a bad relationship. Of course, there's a negative consequence to his avoidance. By playing it so safe, he prevents himself from achieving his dream and experiencing the joys of a happy marriage and family life.

Exercise: Identify Your Worry Behaviors

Now it's your turn to identify your worry behaviors. The next time you worry notice carefully how you react. Did you perform any behaviors like the ones listed above? What were they? List these behaviors in your notebook. You'll focus on these behaviors as you change your response to worry.

Eliminating Worry Behaviors

The idea that changing worry behaviors helps you control your distress dates back to 1966, when psychologist Victor Meyer worked at a hospital in England for people suffering from obsessive-compulsive disorder (OCD). At the time, OCD was considered largely untreatable. At Meyer's hospital, his patients suffered from obsessive fears of contamination, a common form of OCD. In response to those fears, these patients washed themselves excessively. People with this form of OCD can wash their hands hundreds of times a day and take showers that last several hours. Since treatment options were limited at that time, Meyer decided to try a bold cure. He prevented the patients from doing their rituals by shutting off the water in the hospital. Suddenly, because of Meyer's intervention, his patients were unable to wash at all! Yet, remarkably, after an initial rise in anxiety, most of these patients improved significantly. In fact, many experienced relief from their symptoms for the first time in years (Meyer 1966).

The results of Meyer's therapeutic intervention were so encouraging that top researchers such as Edna Foa (Foa and Franklin 2001) and Gail Steketee (1993) took his treatment approach and expanded it to what is now known as exposure and response prevention therapy (ERP). This form of cognitive behavioral therapy is considered the gold standard for treatment of OCD. The principle behind ERP is simple: *Exposure* means confronting your fears and *response prevention* means eliminating any behaviors that reduce your fears, such as washing or checking.

Since worry behaviors and compulsions share many similarities, researchers and clinicians have recently started applying response prevention to the treatment of worry (Brown, O'Leary, and Barlow 2001). The concept is the same as in the treatment of OCD. When you're faced with a worry, refuse to act on it. Eliminate your worry behaviors instead. Like Meyer's patients, you might feel more anxious initially. However, over time your anxiety will decrease, giving you more control over your worry.

COSTS AND BENEFITS OF ELIMINATING WORRY BEHAVIORS

Using response prevention to eliminate your worry behaviors has significant benefits. However, there are also costs to this strategy. It's important to consider both the pros and cons before committing to ridding yourself of these behaviors. The costs of eliminating worry behaviors generally fall into two categories:

1. Temporarily increased anxiety

2. The perceived risk that your fear is more likely to come true

As you can see, the above costs take the form of an increase in short-term discomfort. In contrast, the benefits of eliminating worry behaviors involve reduction of worry in the long term. Here are some of the typical benefits of putting an end to worry behaviors:

- Less anxiety and worry over the long term
- A greater sense of control over your worry
- Freedom from these time-consuming activities
- Improved relationships with other people
- The realization that your fear doesn't come true because it's improbable, not because of these behaviors

---

Exercise: Conduct a Cost-Benefit Analysis

Before you decide to eliminate your worry behaviors, conduct a cost-benefit analysis. Divide a sheet of paper down the middle and list the pros and cons of resisting these behaviors the next time you worry. As you review your list, which side wins? Is it more to your benefit to continue these behaviors or to eliminate them?

CHANGE THE WAY YOU REACT

Let's assume you've decided to use response prevention to eliminate your worry behaviors. Will it really help? Remember Julie, the physical therapist who worried that her son would die in his sleep? She conquered her fear using only this step. At night when her worry hit, instead of checking on her son she stayed in bed. She stubbornly refused to get up and check on him. The first night was extremely difficult. She literally lay in bed gripped with fear. Thoughts of her child dying swamped her mind. But she held her ground and didn't check on him. The next night she did the same thing and her worry started to decrease. In the span of a week, by simply not checking on her son in the middle of the night she defeated a fear that had plagued her for over eight years, ever since he was born.

As you can see from the above example, this step involves taking some risks. One of the main things you risk is that your fear might actually come true. This is extremely unlikely. Julie's son lived because he was healthy and safe and because it's highly unusual for a child to die for no reason in his sleep.

Similarly, many of the things you worry about haven't occurred because they are most likely rare events, not because you've prevented them with your worry behaviors. Nevertheless, it still *feels* risky when you resist these behaviors in the face of worry. Only by eliminating your worry behaviors will you convince yourself that they are unnecessary.

The second thing you risk is the fear that you'll be crippled by the temporarily increased anxiety you feel because of resisting these behaviors. Many people who worry fear that too much anxiety can have catastrophic consequences, such as a nervous breakdown or a psychotic episode. Some of our patients have told us they're afraid that if their anxiety gets too high they'll have to spend the rest of their life in an institution. While this is a common fear, anxiety—no matter how intense—does not cause people to go insane.

Finally, by eliminating worry behaviors, you risk living a life that feels a bit more uncertain. Worry behaviors give the illusion of certainty. You feel that by completing them, you control the outcome of events. If you rid yourself of them, life might seem more uncertain and out of control. But is it really? Or have you lived with uncertainty all along?

Exercise: Eliminate Your Worry Behaviors

Now it's your turn to give this step a try. The next time you catch yourself worrying, *refuse* to do anything about it! You might feel your anxiety rise higher and higher. Be stubborn and don't give in! Eventually, your anxiety will go down and you'll feel better. When this happens, congratulate yourself. You've just taken an important step in conquering your worry.

IF YOU HAVE TROUBLE

Getting rid of your worry behaviors sounds simple, but it's a challenging task. Here are some tips if you have difficulty:

- Eliminate all worry behaviors. Getting rid of some but not others won't have much of an impact on your worry.

- When you eliminate a worry behavior, make sure you don't substitute a new one. This includes new behaviors that serve the same function as the one you eliminated. For instance, if Julie replaced checking on her son with using a baby monitor to listen to him breathe from her bedroom, she wouldn't have truly conquered her fear.

- Get rid of worry behaviors in all situations and at all times. Once you decide to do away with a worry behavior, do so completely. Engaging in the behavior even sporadically will maintain your worry.

- Be suspicious of your actions. Worry behaviors can be remarkably subtle. If you eliminate a worry behavior and don't feel some increase in anxiety initially, you're probably missing something. Look closely. Is there anything you are overlooking? If so, eliminate it.

Replacing Worry Behaviors

Worry behaviors can take up a significant amount of time. Once you've eliminated these behaviors, you might have an abundance of free time, which can be a breeding ground for more worry. Fortunately, there's a solution to this problem—activity scheduling.

Activity scheduling means purposely planning activities to fill your free time. The types of activities you can schedule can be broken down into two categories—*pleasant events* and *mastery events* (Burns 1999a). Pleasant events are activities that you find fun and enjoyable. Here are some examples:

- Shopping
- Reading
- Going to a movie, concert, sporting event, or show
- Having lunch with a friend
- Listening to music

Mastery events are activities that aren't necessarily fun but instead give some sense of satisfaction or accomplishment. Here are some examples:

- Paying bills
- Balancing your checkbook
- Cleaning
- Getting your car fixed
- Updating your résumé
- Exercising

Exercise: List Activities That Are Pleasant or Give You a Sense of Mastery

In your notebook, divide a sheet of paper down the middle. On one side, write the heading "Pleasure," and on the other side, write "Mastery." On the pleasure side, list activities that you enjoy—either now or at some point in the past. Also list activities you think you'd enjoy but have never actually tried. For example, let's say you want to learn to paint. In that case, you'd list painting in the pleasure column even though you've never done it. On the mastery side, list chores and activities that give you a sense of accomplishment when completed. Be sure to list anything you've been putting off, such as seeing your doctor or returning a phone call, on the mastery side as well.

Exercise: Schedule Activities That Are Pleasant or Give You a Sense of Mastery

Once you've listed activities that will bring you pleasure or a sense of mastery, fill out a daily schedule and plug these activities into time slots throughout your day. Pay particular attention to the times you normally worry and do worry behaviors. Schedule activities that will bring you pleasure or a sense of mastery during these times instead and complete them as scheduled.

Key Points

- Worry behaviors reduce anxiety and momentarily make you feel better. Anything that you do in response to worry could be considered a worry behavior.

- Worry behaviors continue because when you engage in them you experience temporary relief. However, in the long run they maintain your worry by validating your fears and by preventing you from discovering that your worries probably won't come true even without them.

- Tracking your responses to worry will help you determine your own set of worry behaviors.

- Eliminating your worry behaviors permanently is a key step in conquering worry. Continuing these behaviors, even sporadically, can maintain your worry.

- Once you've eliminated a worry behavior, you can fill any extra free time by scheduling activities that give you a sense of pleasure or mastery. Pay particular attention to times when you worry or perform worry behaviors and fill those times with enjoyable or productive activities instead.

6

Accept Uncertainty

Most of the solutions described in this book consist of clear, specific steps designed to reduce worry. This chapter is a little different. Instead of suggesting a clear action that directly quells worry, in this chapter we'll ask you to evaluate and modify your philosophy about a key component of worry—uncertainty. We'll explain the role that uncertainty plays in worry and how intolerance of uncertainty lies at the core of worry. We'll also discuss the key factors that interact with intolerance of uncertainty and indirectly result in the maintenance and escalation of worries. We'll describe techniques to address those factors so you can reduce the amount of worry in your life by learning to accept uncertainty.

What Is Uncertainty?

What do we mean by "uncertainty"? Uncertainty is the state that exists when the outcome of something is unclear. If you think about it, this means anything in life. In fact, everything you face on a daily basis is uncertain. Take something small, like eating. How do you know—truly *know*—that you won't choke to death on your next bite? Of course, you don't know for sure. But you still eat. How do you know that the next time you shower, you won't slip and hit your head? You don't, yet you still shower. How do you know that when you step outside in the morning, gravity will still exist? You can't know for certain, but you still leave the house each morning without your spacesuit. Living with uncertainty is something you do on a minute-by-minute basis in your life.

So uncertainty by itself isn't the real issue at the heart of worry. The issue is that you've selected specific areas—your health, relationships, or work, for example—in which you *demand* certainty. You feel you must know how things will turn out. The trouble is you can't. No one has a crystal ball. Could you get fired? Sure. Could you die from some rare illness? It happens. Uncertainty itself is not the problem, as we all live with these possibilities every day. So what is it about uncertainty that leads to worry?

Worry and Intolerance of Uncertainty

Researchers working to untangle the role of uncertainty in worry have identified *intolerance of uncertainty* as a core component of worry and even suggest that this intolerance may be a causal risk factor for worry (Ladouceur, Gosselin, and Dugas 2000). What is intolerance of uncertainty? It can be defined as the tendency to react negatively on an emotional, cognitive, or behavioral level to uncertain situations and events (Dugas, Buhr, and Ladouceur 2004). For example, Dugas and his colleagues noted that high intolerance of uncertainty leads to more concern about ambiguous situations and that worriers are more likely to make threatening interpretations of those unclear situations (Dugas et al. 2005).

This group also found that some people—amazingly—would prefer a known negative outcome to uncertainty. It may seem hard to believe, but we've found the same phenomenon in our practices. One patient even swore that he would rather die tomorrow than live with uncertainty about the effectiveness of the treatment for his medical condition. These strong beliefs about the need for certainty are amply evident in many of our worried clients: What if the electricity goes out during my dinner party tomorrow? The probability is low, but it is still a concern because it *could* happen. My financial situation is fine now, but what if I lose my job? Things are going okay, but that *may* change.

People who suffer from worry—and thus demand certainty—generally assume that uncertain outcomes will be bad. For worriers, it's as if there are no positive surprises in life. As an example, one of our patients got extremely anxious while waiting for the results of a tissue biopsy taken from his dog. During the wait, the outcome, naturally, was uncertain. This patient was absolutely convinced the test result would bring bad news. It was as if that were the only possibility—in fact, you could say he was "certain" his dog was terminally ill. When the possibility of a benign test result was raised, he looked puzzled. It was as if he'd never considered that as an option.

In essence, worriers see uncertainty as negative and something to be avoided at all costs. The trouble is, as we discussed earlier, uncertainty is everywhere. How can you avoid something that is a normal part of life?

But Isn't Uncertainty Bad?

You may be thinking at this point that uncertainty *is* bad—that it's something that you shouldn't tolerate. You may think that seeking certainty—in any situation—is always a good thing. But this is not the case. One of our patients, Dana, related a story about the drawbacks of certainty. She told a story about one Christmas Eve when she was a child. She and her older sister snuck into her parents' closet to find their hidden gifts. They carefully unwrapped each present until they could see what was inside and then rewrapped the gifts. On Christmas morning, they knew exactly what every present was before they opened it. All Dana felt that morning was guilt and sadness—guilt for violating her parents' trust and sadness for a Christmas with no surprises.

Suppose you knew for sure all the positives that would happen in your life. Wouldn't that take away some of the richness and joy? Suppose you knew for sure all the negatives in your life in advance. Wouldn't that put a damper on it? Would you ever date your first love, knowing you'll ultimately break up? Would you ever scratch off a lottery ticket, knowing you won't win? Would you ever root for your hometown football team, knowing they'll blow it by missing a last-second field goal?

It's uncertainty—the thrill of *not* knowing—that allows us to get caught up in life and feel romance, excitement, joy, and wonder. When we give up the need to know, life becomes vibrant and, yes, a little risky. Without some uncertainty, life is dull and boring—like knowing what your gifts are before you open them. A life without uncertainty would leave no possibility of pleasant surprises, and negative outcomes known in advance would eliminate the desire to take any risks.

How to Tackle Your Intolerance of Uncertainty

Since uncertainty exists in everything we do, the goal is not to eliminate it but to recognize and accept it as an inevitable part of life. We cannot get rid of uncertain situations, but we can develop coping strategies to deal with them. Studies have found that cognitive behavioral interventions similar to those described in this book are successful in improving tolerance of uncertainty and decreasing worry (Ladouceur, Dugas, et al. 2000). But successfully targeting intolerance of uncertainty also involves addressing the following key variables that interact with it to produce and maintain worry:

- Erroneous positive beliefs about worry

- Cognitive avoidance

- Negative problem orientation

In the following sections, we'll describe techniques to help you tackle these factors related to uncertainty. We'll also help you to identify which strategies work best with which worry types.

IDENTIFY THE WORRY TYPE

As we discussed previously, worry can actually serve a useful function—some types of worry, that is. Productive worry leads us to make decisions, make changes in our lives, or better prepare for tasks or situations. Unfortunately, much of our worry tends to be future-oriented and unproductive. Unproductive worry is focused on things we can't control or problems that don't even exist and may never occur. It is often difficult for worriers to tell the difference. The result is that all worries seem important, probable, and necessary.

As you know, productive worry can be distinguished from unproductive worry by considering such issues as time frame (present versus future), plausibility, and possibility for immediate action (Leahy 2004). Why is it important to learn to identify the difference between productive and unproductive worries? Because the strategies you'll use to address worries about current and plausible problems will be different than those used to deal with future-oriented, unlikely worries.

Exercise: Identify the Type of Worry

Practice distinguishing between productive and unproductive worry with the examples listed below. Which are productive? Which are unproductive? Recall that productive worries are those that are realistic, current, and controllable, while unproductive worries are unrealistic, future-oriented, and out of your control.

What if I'm not prepared for my presentation next week?

- ☐ Realistic, current, controllable
- ☐ Unrealistic, future-oriented, out of your control

What if I get brain cancer and die?

- ☐ Realistic, current, controllable
- ☐ Unrealistic, future-oriented, out of your control

What if my plane crashes?

- ☐ Realistic, current, controllable
- ☐ Unrealistic, future-oriented, out of your control

What if I fail my test?

- ☐ Realistic, current, controllable
- ☐ Unrealistic, future-oriented, out of your control

What if my daughter gets the bird flu?

- ☐ Realistic, current, controllable
- ☐ Unrealistic, future-oriented, out of your control

What if my spouse dies in a car accident?

- ☐ Realistic, current, controllable
- ☐ Unrealistic, future-oriented, out of your control

What if my car breaks down?

- ☐ Realistic, current, controllable
- ☐ Unrealistic, future-oriented, out of your control

What if I can't think of anything to say at the party?

- ☐ Realistic, current, controllable
- ☐ Unrealistic, future-oriented, out of your control

How did you do? Were you able to identify which thoughts were current and plausible and which were future-oriented and unrealistic? If you had trouble, consider these questions: Is this likely to happen? Are there any possible solutions to the problem? Is there anything that you could do about it today to make a change? How about within the next week? If the answer to these questions is no, it is likely an unproductive or future-oriented worry. In the above exercise, concerns about brain cancer, a plane crash, losing your spouse in a car accident, and bird flu are examples of worry that's unproductive, future-oriented, and out of your control.

REEVALUATE YOUR POSITIVE BELIEFS ABOUT WORRY

Now that you've practiced distinguishing between current, productive worries and improbable, future-oriented worries, it's time to take a look at your beliefs about your worries. If you're like other worriers, you have a love-hate relationship with your worry. You may dislike the anxiety and stress your worry causes you, but you may hold several positive beliefs about your worry as well (Wells 1999). Here are some common positive beliefs about worry:

- **Worry helps me find solutions to my problems.** If you hold this belief, you might wonder, "How will I be prepared for possible problems if I don't consider all the possible outcomes?"

- **Worry motivates me to do things.** This belief is often stated as "If I didn't worry about these things, then they would never get done."

- **Worry protects me from negative emotions.** One of our patients accurately captured the essence of this belief with this simple statement: "I'd rather worry about it now than be surprised when the 'other shoe drops.'"

- **Worry prevents negative outcomes.** You may believe, for example, that "If I don't worry about becoming ill, something bad may happen."

- **Worrying means I'm a conscientious, responsible person.** As an example, you may express this belief by asking, "What kind of a person would I be if I didn't worry about my kids?"

So what does this have to do with uncertainty? Some researchers hypothesize that intolerance of uncertainty actually contributes to the development of these positive beliefs through the process of reinforcement (Dugas, Buhr, and Ladouceur 2004).

For instance, if you're intolerant of uncertainty you may develop the belief that worry will protect you from negative emotions in the future. In other words, if you worry "in advance," then you'll never be disappointed or surprised when something bad happens. This belief would encourage you to worry and would maintain your intolerance of uncertainty by never allowing you to learn that you could deal with unwanted surprises without advanced preparation.

Exercise: Challenge Your Beliefs About Worry

Use the following questions to help you challenge your positive beliefs about worry. By challenging these beliefs, you'll find it easier to let go of worry and, ultimately, your need for certainty:

- Am I better at solving problems because of my worry? What evidence do I have for this idea?

- Are there any times when I've dealt with an unexpected crisis effectively even though I didn't worry about it ahead of time?

- Do I concentrate better or worse when I'm anxious and worried? Does this help me generate solutions for my problems? Does it improve my productivity?

- Does my worry ever keep me from completing a project or task because

- When bad things have happened in the past, did they still make me sad, scared, or angry—even though I worried about them beforehand?

- Have good events happened out of the blue, even if I hadn't thought about or planned for them? Have bad things taken place even though I worried about them ahead of time?

- Do I have friends or family members who worry less than I do? Does that mean they are cold or uncaring people?

Write the answers to these questions in your notebook and review them anytime you find it difficult to dismiss your worries or whenever you feel your unproductive worry is actually useful.

BEWARE OF COGNITIVE AVOIDANCE

Another variable that interacts with intolerance of uncertainty to create worry is *cognitive avoidance* (Dugas, Buhr, and Ladouceur 2004). People who have difficulty tolerating uncertainty may use worry in an attempt to anticipate negative outcomes. Because they tend to do this using verbal thoughts rather than images (Borkovec and Inz 1990), it also becomes a way to avoid threatening mental images of feared future catastrophes.

In this way, worry allows avoidance of these distressing images of uncertain future outcomes or feared catastrophes. But avoidance also tends to make the catastrophic thoughts stronger by reinforcing their importance and by undermining your confidence in your ability to tolerate the uncertain outcome of the things you worry about. Because future-oriented problems cannot be addressed using regular problem-solving skills—you can't fix what hasn't happened yet—these problems are best addressed using a method called *worry exposure*. This strategy will be discussed in more detail in chapter 9.

OVERCOME NEGATIVE PROBLEM ORIENTATION

The final factor that interacts with intolerance of uncertainty to create worry is a negative problem orientation. While the ability to solve problems is intact in worriers, they tend to have difficulty *applying* these skills. *Problem orientation* refers to how you think and feel about your problems as well as how you assess your problem-solving skills. Researchers have found that a negative problem orientation is clearly associated with worry (Dugas and Ladouceur 2000).

Because the outcome of any problem is uncertain, it's easy to see how worriers, who find it difficult to tolerate uncertainty, would have a tendency to focus on these uncertain aspects rather than solutions. But, although some researchers have found that patients with generalized anxiety disorder have less confidence in their problem-solving ability than nonworriers (Dugas et al. 1998), the good news is that there are no differences in ability to solve problems. You *can* use your problem-solving skills to address productive worries.

Exercise: Use Your Problem-Solving Skills

Pick a worry from your notebook that you think fits the criteria of a productive worry—one that is plausible, current, and solvable. Now take that worry and go through the following steps:

1. Define the key elements of the problem. Be as specific as possible. Be sure to also write what you would like to be different.

2. Write down every possible solution you can generate. Include any possible options, no matter how silly they may seem.

3. Now pick the solution that you think has the best chance of success and that seems most workable.

4. Break down that solution into any smaller steps needed to achieve the goal.

5. Go do it!

You may find that this process is tedious or difficult at first. But with practice, you'll be able to go through the process much more efficiently and effectively. Over time, you'll develop more confidence in your ability to use your problem-solving skills, and you may even find that you're able to eliminate some of the worries on your list.

LEARN TO TOLERATE UNCERTAINTY

Now it's time to take what you've learned in this chapter and use it to help you fully experience the uncertainty of life. Use the statements below to respond to your what-if thinking:

- I'll never know for sure.

- Maybe it will, maybe it won't.

- I can't predict the future.

- I'll cope with things as they happen.

- Risk is a part of life—nothing ventured, nothing gained.

- I can't be absolutely certain either way.

- Anything is possible.

The next time you find yourself faced with a what-if question, resist the temptation to answer it. Resist the desire to seek certainty in the face of the unknown, and instead accept what is real—that you truly don't know for sure. Allow uncertainty into your mind and accept the doubt that is inherent in life.

Key Points

- Intolerance of uncertainty plays a key role in worry.

- Variables such as positive beliefs about worry, cognitive avoidance, and poor problem orientation may interact with intolerance of uncertainty to produce and maintain worry.

- Many worriers have positive beliefs about their worry, and challenging these beliefs may be beneficial in reducing worry.

- Future-oriented or unproductive worry may be best confronted through worry exposure.

- Worriers have less confidence in their ability to solve problems and more difficulty applying these skills, despite having intact problem-solving abilities.

- Current or plausible worries can be addressed using your problem-solving skills.

- Consider the role of uncertainty in your life and practice your ability to accept and experience uncertainty.

7

Manage Your Time

We all occasionally feel as though there are just too many things to do and not nearly enough time to do them. However, without effective time management skills, obligations and duties feel overwhelming all too often. Inefficient use of time can cause frustration, procrastination, stress, worry, and decreased productivity. Can you think of times in the past month when you rushed to finish a project or a task? Were there times that you didn't do something important because you couldn't find the time?

The good news is that you can learn to control your time—even if it doesn't feel that way. And doing so will have a positive impact on your worry. Research has shown that building time management skills decreases avoidance, procrastination, and worry (Van Eerde 2003). There *is* enough time to finish tasks, meet goals, and do the things you want—if you improve your time management. In this chapter, we'll show you how to manage your time better—and decrease your worry as a result.

Effective Time Management

Below we'll describe an effective time management approach. This strategy consists of four steps:

1. Developing awareness

2. Analyzing how you spend your time

3. Planning your time

4. Evaluating your plan

STEP ONE: DEVELOPING AWARENESS

Most people think that they have a handle on where their time goes but are unaware of time wasted on unnecessary or unproductive tasks. Before you can improve how you spend your time, first look at what you're doing with it now using the following steps:

1. At the top of a new page in your notebook, write tomorrow's day and date. Along the left side of the page, divide the day into fifteen-minute intervals beginning at 6:00 a.m. Be sure to include all twenty-four hours. Now, do the same thing for each day of the upcoming week.

2. Now you're ready to begin recording how you currently spend your time. For the next week, closely monitor your activities. This will give you a detailed idea of where you spend your time and if adjustments might help. Be sure to keep track of how much time you spend sleeping, eating, commuting, watching television, and running errands. Be as detailed as possible. Keep your notebook with you and record activities as soon as you complete them. Don't rely on your memory or wait until the end of the day to fill

out the form. For this exercise to be useful, you need an accurate picture of your schedule.

3. You might feel like you don't need to do this because you already know how you spend your time. As an experiment, write down your estimates of how much time you'll spend doing the activities listed above during the next week. Then, monitor your time for at least a few days and see how close your guesses were. Our patients usually find they weren't very accurate in their estimates. In fact, they're often shocked at the amount of time they spend on things like commuting or watching TV.

Does keeping such close track of your schedule sound overwhelming to you? Do you feel like you don't have the time to do it? Keep in mind, this is only temporary. You don't have to do this exercise for the rest of your life, just one week. And by spending the time now, you'll gain more time in the future. Consider it an investment in decreasing your worry and stress and as the first step to gaining more control over how you use your time.

STEP TWO: ANALYZING HOW YOU SPEND YOUR TIME

Did you record your activities for the week? If not, do so before you move on. It's an essential step in managing your time better. By recording your activities, you can look at where your time went. Once you've recorded your activities, analyze how you spent your time using the following steps:

1. Look at the activities you recorded over the past week. Can you group them into categories? Write these categories in a column along the left side of a new page in your notebook. Some possibilities include sleeping, eating, working,

reading, watching TV, running errands, making phone calls, personal grooming or hygiene, cooking meals, caring for children, doing household chores, commuting, and recreation. Use these categories as a start, but add anything to the list that fits for you.

2. Now, on the right side of that page, tally up how much time you spent over the past week doing activities in each category. Be sure that you account for all the hours in a week: 168.

3. Were you surprised by anything? Did you spend more time on anything than you thought you would? Was there anything you wish you'd done more of? How about less of? Was there anything you could have delegated to someone else or said no to? Did you spend any time doing unnecessary tasks? Did you notice anything that you wish you'd spent more time on? Anything that you wanted to get done but didn't? Record your answers to these questions in your notebook.

Andrea was a patient who used this step to reduce her worry. As a business executive with a hectic schedule, one of her main complaints was her inability to manage time effectively. As she went through her day, she frequently felt anxious and overwhelmed by the sheer number of tasks facing her. In an effort to improve her time management skills, and bring her worry under control, Andrea monitored her activities for one week. She then tallied up the amount of time she spent on each type of activity. She discovered that many tasks took much longer than necessary. This gave her hope that she could manage her time more effectively. By following the next two steps, she recaptured lost time and reevaluated her priorities. As a result, she was able to spend more time on things that were important to her. These new skills helped Andrea dramatically reduce her worry.

STEP THREE: PLANNING YOUR TIME

The next step is making a plan for how you'd like to spend your time. Take a look at how you answered the questions in step two and consider those answers when planning your upcoming week. Did you spend your time in a manner consistent with your priorities or goals? If you found that you spent a lot of time in activities that were unnecessary while other important tasks went undone, the following strategy might help. Use the steps below to determine the most effective way to spend your time:

1. In your notebook, make a blank schedule similar to the one you used when you recorded your weekly activities.

2. Divide your days into fifteen-minute blocks. Then go through and write in any scheduled appointments, meetings, or other activities that have a firm beginning and ending time.

3. Next, record times for sleeping, eating, commuting, and any other necessary daily tasks like grooming or personal hygiene. Make sure you're realistic about the amount of time these activities take.

4. Use the remaining time slots for optional tasks or goals that may vary on a day-to-day basis. Since these tasks are optional, you must prioritize them in some way to ensure that the important and urgent things get done in a timely manner and that unimportant things don't interfere with this process.

To prioritize effectively, first make a master list of things you want to accomplish. You can add to this list as new goals or obligations arise. Think about each task on your list and whether it falls into one of the following categories:

- **High priority:** extremely important and critical to complete today

- **Medium priority:** very important, but not urgent that it be done today

- **Low priority:** important and needs to be done, but not right away

If any tasks don't fit into one of these categories—if they are unimportant or unnecessary—consider crossing them off your list altogether. Or ask yourself if any of these tasks could be delegated to a coworker or family member. If so, do it! For the tasks that remain, make a notation next to each one indicating whether it's high, medium, or low priority. Now look at your schedule for the week and take high-priority items from your master list and put them into the free slots in your schedule. If any free time remains, take medium-priority tasks from the list and schedule them. Schedule low-priority tasks only if time remains after you've accounted for high- and medium-priority tasks.

Tips for Successful Scheduling

As you practice scheduling your time more productively, you may run into a few problems. Here are some additional tips to ensure your planning is as effective as possible:

- Be realistic in your estimates of how long activities will take you. When in doubt, allow for extra time.

- Leave time between tasks so you don't rush from one thing to the next. Pause to relax and reflect for a few minutes after you've completed an activity.

- Allow for travel time and always plan for the most likely scenario. Avoid scheduling only the amount of time that it takes you to get somewhere under ideal weather or traffic conditions.

- Leave some flexibility in your schedule for emergencies or unexpected high-priority tasks.

- Whenever possible, finish one activity before moving on to the next. Leaving a bunch of tasks partially completed contributes to worry and interferes with your long-term productivity.

- Plan clear start and stop times. Projects have a way of expanding to fill the amount of time available. Clear ending times can be motivating and increase your focus and efficiency.

- Don't forget to schedule time for yourself! Remember that making room for downtime and recreation or hobbies is important too. In the long run, you'll be more productive if you allow some time for yourself.

STEP FOUR: EVALUATING YOUR PLAN

In order to evaluate your plan, you need to keep track of how closely you stick to it. For the next week or two, make an extra column to the right of your planned activities and monitor what you actually did with your time. How well did you do? Did you complete your high-priority tasks? If so, congratulations! Take a moment and give yourself credit—you just took a step to reduce your worry. If you didn't complete important tasks, ask yourself why. What prevented you from sticking to your plan? Did you engage in low-priority or unnecessary tasks and neglect important ones? If so, you might find the next section helpful.

Dealing with Procrastination

Procrastination is a trap we all fall into at one time or another. In fact, one of the most common problems our patients report is procrastination. Who hasn't put off an unpleasant project or task in favor of something more appealing? Who has never waited until the last minute to prepare for a meeting or a class? We all do it because it works—at least in the short term—by letting us avoid something that's unpleasant or provokes anxiety. However, there's a cost in the end. Studies have found that procrastination is actually associated with increased worry (Stöber and Joorman 2001). So in the long run, putting things off may actually cause you more discomfort and stress than facing those tasks right away.

WHY DO PEOPLE PROCRASTINATE?

Many explanations exist for why people put things off. Look at your schedule over the past week and see if you can find any times that you procrastinated or avoided a task that needed your attention. Read the following list and see if any of these reasons for procrastinating apply to you:

- **Fear of failure:** Sometimes people put off tasks because they are fearful that they won't succeed at them. In their mind, not finishing a project or doing a poor job because they ran out of time is less painful than the possibility of failing after putting forth full effort.

- **Perfectionism:** People may set standards for a task that are simply too high. Feeling that a project or task needs to be perfect may actually prevent it from getting done at all.

- **Overestimating the task:** Tasks can seem daunting at times. But often people overestimate how long a particular task will take or how difficult it will be to complete. It then becomes easier to put it off or not do it at all.

- **Worrying about it:** Rather than working on a project and making progress toward completion, many people spend time worrying about it. In this way, you waste your time on worry instead of using it productively.

- **Taking too much responsibility:** Taking too much responsibility for the outcome of a project can be paralyzing, leaving you frozen and avoiding the task instead of working productively on it.

OVERCOMING PROCRASTINATION

Did any of those reasons for procrastination apply to you? If so, look at the strategies below and use them to overcome procrastination. Remember, in the long run, putting things off only causes more anxiety and worry. Take control of your time and begin crossing things off your list!

- **Address any negative beliefs about failure.** What is the likelihood that if you try you will fail? And what would actually happen if you gave it a try and didn't succeed? Do you know anyone who has never failed? Look at your feared consequences and ask yourself, objectively, if they are likely to happen. Would the feared outcome be any worse than not doing the task at all? If not, then give it a try.

- **Banish perfectionism.** Do you find that you don't get things done either because you spend too much time trying to make them perfect or because, by wanting them to be perfect, you never do them at all? If so, ask yourself what would happen if they weren't perfect? What would that mean to you? What would that say about you? It may be difficult, but in order to get past the obstacle of perfectionism you will need to test out your beliefs. Practice turning in assignments with small errors, stop cleaning the kitchen before you feel the job is completely done, or return phone calls that aren't urgent the next day rather than immediately. Then look at what happened. Did anything turn out differently as a result? If not, practice being imperfect some more!

- **Break it down into steps.** Tasks often seem so overwhelming that it's difficult to know where to begin. If you notice that you often procrastinate because you don't know where to start, consider each project or task as a series of small steps rather than as an overwhelming whole. For instance, if you need to purchase new car insurance, you may break that down into the steps of reading about different insurance companies on the Internet, finding phone numbers of local agents for those companies, and requesting estimates from them. When you make your schedule, list these steps rather than the entire project as your goal. This will increase your productivity, and before you know it, you'll complete the whole task.

- **Don't worry; take action.** If you find that you spend more time worrying about a task than actually performing it, it's often best to just dive right in. You'll find that once you get started, not only does the task go more quickly than you thought, it's often less unpleasant than you expected. Remember, worrying about it only prolongs the anxiety. By getting started right away, you'll be more productive and you'll spend less time thinking about unpleasant tasks. Plus, as a bonus, you'll have more time to do the things you want to do.

- **Consider how you'll feel when the task is complete.** If you still find you have trouble diving right in, envision how you'll feel and what you'll do when the task is complete. What fun things will you be able to do when you're finished? How will finishing a task you've put off affect your anxiety or stress level? If you need to, list the pros and cons of doing the task now rather than waiting until later. But don't spend too much time convincing yourself. Remember, the best strategy is still to do it now!

- **Tell everyone your goal.** Publicly announce your intentions. Tell your boss, your roommate, your spouse, your friend—anyone who will listen. By doing so, you not only increase your motivation to achieve your goal, you also enlist the support and assistance of others. Encourage others to check in with you on your progress. If you run into obstacles, ask for help in figuring out good ways to meet your goal. And, most importantly, invite others to celebrate with you when you finish your project!

Key Points

- Poor use of time leads to increased frustration, anxiety, and worry. Time management training has been shown to reduce these negative feelings, including worry.

- Many people aren't aware of how they spend their time. Increasing your awareness of how you use your time is the first step to better time management.

- Planning and prioritizing tasks more effectively improves productivity and decreases anxiety and worry.

- Procrastination is a common problem that you can overcome by looking closely at why you put things off and implementing strategies that address those reasons.

8

Communicate Assertively

As you've probably experienced, the demands of life are not always reasonable or fair. There is plenty to worry about in life, but taking on too much responsibility, always yielding to demands, and not standing up for your rights can lead to increased anxiety and worry. Poor communication skills can cause you to avoid intimate relationships, affect your productivity at work, and result in undue stress and worry. In this chapter, you'll learn how to identify different communication styles, how to assertively communicate your feelings and needs to others, and how to refuse unreasonable requests.

How Communication Affects Worry

Worriers often grow up with the belief that the needs of others are more important than their own. Perhaps you learned that you should accommodate others whenever possible, or maybe that you should keep complaints to yourself or never question authority. While this may allow you to move through life with little conflict or disagreement with others, the downside is that it wears on you over time and may lead you to feel angry, hurt, resentful, or ineffective. You can only maintain this type of behavior for so long before built-up frustration and anxiety lead you to blow up at your spouse, your boss, or some unsuspecting stranger. Worse yet, you may turn these frustrations inward and find that carrying these unexpressed feelings and chronic burdens wrecks your physical and mental well-being over time. Luckily, there is a middle ground between blowing up and giving in. It's called *assertiveness*.

Assertiveness means expressing your personal rights while simultaneously respecting the rights of others (Lange and Jakubowski 1976). By learning to communicate assertively, you can reduce a major source of stress and worry—your relationships with other people. To fully understand assertiveness, though, you need to first learn about the other types of communication.

Aggressive: People with an aggressive style of communication often disregard the needs and feelings of others in favor of their own. They may yell, threaten, accuse, or belittle to get their way. They tend to indiscriminately roll over others en route to meeting their desires. This method works at times, as other people may give in to aggressive communicators to prevent a fight or to avoid an unpleasant interaction. However, the downside is that this communication style often leads to being disliked, feared, or avoided.

Passive: On the opposite end of the spectrum, passive communicators will do anything to avoid confrontation or disagreements. They always put the needs of others ahead of their own and never stand up for their rights. Because they allow other people to walk all over them, they avoid experiencing arguments or disapproval. However, rarely can someone consistently fail to express their feelings without eventually feeling angry, frustrated, stressed, or resentful.

Assertive: Assertive communicators fall somewhere in between aggressive and passive, in an ideal spot where the rights of others are respected while personal needs are also met. These communicators will stand up for their rights and express their feelings while also being considerate and respectful of others. The benefits of communicating in this way are that others don't take advantage of you, and your needs are met without alienating others. Assertive communication is the most effective method of interacting with other people.

Exercise: Identify Communication Styles

Now that you've learned the three main ways people communicate, see if you can identify the style of interaction in these three scenarios:

1. Maria is in line at the customer service counter and has been waiting for several minutes. When Maria's number is called, a man who has just walked in cuts in front of her and heads to the counter. Maria says, "Sir, I'm not sure if you realize it, but we're being waited on in order of arrival and it's my turn. The numbers to hold your spot in line are over near the door." Is Maria's response aggressive, passive, or assertive? Why?

2. Robert is a copier salesman, and his sales manager has just asked him to trade territories with a coworker. This trade would require that Robert double his travel and do a lot of work to build up as many contacts as he's already established in his current territory. Robert knows this will cause him problems at home because he'll spend even less time with his wife and

kids, but he feels he should be a team player, so he responds, "Certainly, sir." Is Robert's behavior aggressive, passive, or assertive? Why?

3. Michelle comes home from a long day at work to find that her husband hasn't cooked dinner as he promised. Instead, she finds him watching a basketball game on television. Furious, she yells, "You never do anything around here. I might as well be single. We're headed for a divorce, buddy!" Is Michelle's behavior aggressive, passive, or assertive? Why?

How did you do? Did you think that Maria's behavior was appropriately assertive because she stood up for her rights while respecting the rights of others? Did you think that Robert's response was passive and that he didn't express his feelings? Was Michelle aggressive in her reaction to the situation, resorting to yelling and threats to make her point? If so, great! You're on the right track. Understanding the difference between these three types of responses is a big step in learning how to be assertive. If you need to, go back and review the definitions of aggressive, passive, and assertive communication before moving on.

You Can Be More Assertive

In this section, we'll go through the steps of communicating in a more assertive way:

1. Defining the situation

2. Expressing yourself

3. Proposing a solution

4. Outlining the consequences

As you can see from these steps, assertiveness—like any other skill—can be broken down into separate parts. These steps need to be practiced in order to master assertive communication. Communicating more assertively may feel strange at first, but with practice you'll gradually become more comfortable expressing yourself and you'll soon notice a positive change in your relationships and a reduction of stress and worry in your life.

STEP ONE: DEFINING THE SITUATION

According to Bower and Bower's book *Asserting Yourself* (1991), the first step in learning to communicate more assertively is to define the situation or situations in which you have difficulty being assertive. Be as specific as possible. Include *who* is involved, *when* this usually occurs, and *what* is likely to happen. Also include how you usually *respond* and what you would like to see happen differently in the future (*assertive goal*).

For example, Shannon, a single mother, has difficulty being assertive in the following scenario: In the evening after dinner (when), when it was time for her teenage son (who) to do his homework, Shannon often found him in his room watching television or playing video games (what). Shannon would remind him of his homework and, when he didn't respond, would go downstairs to the kitchen and feel sad and helpless and worry about her son's grades (response). This pattern would repeat itself several times each evening. Shannon would like her son to respond to her request promptly or do his homework without being asked (assertive goal).

STEP TWO: EXPRESSING YOURSELF

The next step in learning to communicate assertively is expressing how the situation or the other person's behavior makes you feel. Always remember to use "I" statements when expressing your feelings to avoid casting blame on the other person. "I" statements allow you to state how you feel about a behavior or a situation without accusing or blaming the other person. For example, Shannon might say to her son, "When you don't respond to my requests, I feel like you don't respect me." Or she could say, "You make me feel sad when you don't listen to me." Which of these statements do you think makes appropriate use of "I" statements? Right! The first one includes Shannon's feelings about the situation but doesn't shift responsibility for her emotions to her son.

STEP THREE: PROPOSING A SOLUTION

Next, propose a possible solution to the situation. Be prepared to put forth the solution that you'd like to occur. Be specific and concise in your request. If possible, try to convey your preferred solution as a firm request but not a command. For example, Shannon might say to her son, "From now on, I would like you to do your homework before dinner and before watching any television or playing video games. I will only remind you once each evening."

STEP FOUR: OUTLINING THE CONSEQUENCES

Once you've proposed a possible solution, you can outline the consequences of this new arrangement, beginning with the likely positive outcomes. For example, Shannon could say, "This will allow us to both be satisfied. I'll be content knowing your homework is done. You'll have your time after dinner to do what you'd like and not have me pestering you to finish your assignments." If it doesn't work to highlight the positive consequences of your request, it may be appropriate to set limits or impose negative consequences. For instance, if Shannon's son doesn't agree or comply with this new arrangement, she may need to list the negative outcomes to his behavior. She might say, "If you don't complete your homework before dinner or if I have to remind you more than once to work on it, I will take away your television and game privileges for that evening."

Exercise: Practice Assertive Communication

Remember the steps—define, express, propose, and outline. Do you have them down? Now think about a situation in which you have trouble being assertive. Take out your notebook and write out a detailed account of that situation. Be sure to be specific and to include who is involved, what happens and when, how you normally deal with it, and what you would like to be different, or your goal. Once you've described the situation, go through each of the other steps. How would you express your feelings to the person or persons involved in a nonblaming way, using "I" statements? What would you propose as a solution? What are the potential positive results of this solution and, if necessary, what are the consequences of not agreeing to the solution?

Now repeat this exercise for at least five situations in which you find it difficult to express your feelings, have a hard time saying no, or feel that others take advantage of you.

When Problems Arise

If you think this sounds too good to be true, you're right. Others will not always respond positively to your assertive requests, and you may not always have the time to think through a situation thoroughly before you respond. With practice, however, being assertive will become second nature and you'll respond quickly and with ease. But until then, here are some tips for dealing with challenging situations and difficult people.

WHEN YOU'RE PUT ON THE SPOT

What happens when you feel caught off guard or are too upset to respond assertively in the moment? Remember that not responding *immediately* is not the same as not responding at all. Sometimes the best course of action is to postpone answering until you can collect your thoughts and respond assertively. Remember, it's your right to not answer immediately. Answering too quickly can often get you stuck agreeing to things you really don't want to do or giving a response that you regret later. In this situation, saying "I need to think about that before I can commit" or "I don't really feel able to discuss it at this time" may buy you some time to formulate your assertive response.

WHEN DEALING WITH AN AGGRESSIVE COMMUNICATOR

What do you do when someone is just not playing by the rules of assertive communication? It is quite likely that you'll encounter that situation at one time or another. People may respond to your requests with sarcasm, disdain, or downright hostility. As hard as it may be, don't get caught up in this negativity or take these responses too personally. Remember, it takes at least two people to argue, and no one can make you agree to something that you truly don't want to do.

One way to diffuse such situations is to try to find something that you can agree on with the other person. Even when someone is communicating aggressively, there is usually a bit of truth in what they're saying. It can be helpful to take that bit of truth and acknowledge it.

For example, let's consider the case of Michelle, earlier in this chapter, who told her husband "You never do anything around here!" He could easily respond with "I do more than you" or "How would you know? You're never around anyway," but this is aggressive and would likely lead to more arguing. How could Michelle's husband hear her comment and find some truth in it to avoid further conflict? He might respond, "It's true that I didn't make dinner as I said I would, so I can understand why you're feeling upset, but I do contribute to the household in many ways."

WHEN SOMEONE JUST WON'T LISTEN

Although it may sound silly, when someone is not hearing your request, sometimes the best strategy is to simply repeat your stance until they do. This is known as the "broken record" technique. By repeating your statement, you let the other person know that you cannot be swayed and that arguing will be ineffective. For example, if your supervisor asks you to work on a weekend that you've already requested to have off, what would a good "broken record" response be? For practice, see if you can come up with some effective replies and write them in your notebook.

WHEN ANGER GETS IN THE WAY

When it seems that anger or emotion has taken over the conversation and clouded the message, it may help to take a time-out from the situation using the delaying technique described above. Alternatively, you may choose to call attention to the fact that the discussion has gotten derailed and clarify the issue. For example, you might say something like "You seem really angry right now. Can you tell me what about my request is bothering you so much?" Or, if you already understand why the person is upset, you may choose to show empathy or reflect their feelings back to them. For example, Michelle's husband might have said something like, "I know how hard you work, and I can understand why you may have been upset when I didn't make dinner as I promised." This shows that the other person's feelings are understood and respected, a crucial ingredient to dealing more effectively with people.

WHEN NEEDS ARE INCOMPATIBLE

What happens when someone is not being unreasonable but their needs are in conflict with yours? It is quite possible that you'll encounter such situations, as everyone operates with a different set of needs. In this case, it may be best to acknowledge the discrepancy, listen to the other person's needs, and attempt to devise some sort of compromise.

Key Points

- Poor communication can disrupt relationships and increase anxiety and worry. Improving your communication style can improve your relationships and lessen your worry as a result.

- There are three main types of communication: aggressive, passive, and assertive.

- Assertive communicators respect the rights of others while simultaneously meeting their personal needs.

- The four steps to assertive communication are defining the problem, expressing your feelings, proposing a solution, and outlining the consequences.

- It takes practice to feel comfortable communicating assertively. With time and effort, it becomes second nature.

9 **Confront Your Worries**

How many times has someone told you, "Don't worry, it'll be fine" or "Stop worrying about it, just think positively"? Like most worriers, you've probably heard it more times than you can count. It certainly seems like good advice; if worrying about something is bothering you, then it makes sense to stop thinking about it. So why doesn't it work?

Why Avoidance Is Harmful

There are several reasons avoidance doesn't work, especially for worry. For one, what happens when you try to *not* think about something? Not sure? Try this experiment: For one full minute, try to *not* think about something—a giraffe, a red balloon—pick any object you want. Just, whatever you do, don't think about it! Go ahead, try it now.

How successful were you? If you're like most people, you probably weren't very successful at all. It may even seem that the more you tried to not think about it, the more the object tended to pop into your mind. In fact, some scientific studies have found the same thing: the more we try to suppress thoughts, the more likely they are to occur (Wegman 1994). And even when people are successful, they find it very difficult to maintain this level of concentration for very long—it's exhausting!

But even if you could manage to do it, there are other pitfalls of trying to avoid thoughts that worry or frighten you. While it's human nature to want to avoid things that are unpleasant or that cause discomfort, doing so may actually increase our fears in the long run. This is because by avoiding thoughts that upset you, you acknowledge them as a real threat or danger and as something that should be avoided at all costs. This undermines your confidence in your ability to tolerate these thoughts and to manage your anxiety, which in turn makes the thoughts even more powerful and frightening.

Avoiding thoughts or fears also keeps you from learning that you really could face these thoughts and that nothing bad would happen if you did confront them. Along the same lines, the more you avoid certain worries or situations now, the more likely you are to avoid them in the future, setting up a vicious cycle of anxiety and avoidance.

You may have already guessed where this is going, and it probably sounds fairly unpleasant. If so, you are not alone. Most people are skeptical when they hear that a good way to have fewer worries is to actually worry *more* on purpose. But it's true—by confronting your feared thoughts you take a big step toward controlling your worry. Cognitive behavioral treatment that includes exposure to worrisome thoughts and images has been found by some researchers to produce significant decreases in anxiety, worry, and physical symptoms (Ladouceur, Dugas, et al. 2000). Directly confronting your worries by deliberately exposing yourself to them is known as *worry exposure*.

But I Already Worry All the Time!

Our patients are often leery of doing worry exposures because it seems to them that they already worry constantly. However, if you think about your patterns of worry you may realize that, like most worriers, you rarely settle on one worry at a time. It's common for worries to shift quickly from one to the next. This process is called "chaining," and often it happens so fast that there's no time for individual worries to be objectively evaluated (Zinbarg, Craske, and Barlow 1993). The result is usually escalation of anxiety with each successive thought.

For example, Paula, a busy mother of four, often worried about the amount of time she spent helping her children with their homework. With all of her household responsibilities, she found it difficult to allocate as much time to helping each child as she felt she should. Despite the fact that her children were all doing quite well in school, Paula worried that because she wasn't supervising them closely enough their grades would suffer. She would lie awake in bed at night thinking about how poor grades would lead her children to be rejected from top-notch colleges, how this would damage their self-esteem, and how they would never live up to their true potential. Paula then predicted that they'd probably drop out of college, end up in dead-end jobs and bad relationships, and be destined to a life of unhappiness. As this string of worries flooded her mind, she found that her anxiety would build, making it difficult for her to sleep as she imagined a miserable future for her children.

Part of the reason that Paula became more anxious as she worried is that she wasn't focused on any worry long enough to evaluate it objectively. Sticking with one thought, such as "My kids will get bad grades because I don't help them enough with their homework" would have allowed her to examine the evidence against that thought. For instance, one piece of evidence disputing her thought was that her kids were in fact getting good grades with her current level of involvement.

THE MAGIC OF HABITUATION

Another benefit of sticking with one thought is that the longer you stay with it and focus on it, the less it bothers you. This process is called *habituation*. Research shows that if you engage in focused and repeated exposure to a thought or situation, your anxiety will decrease over time (Foa and Kozak 1986). Distracting yourself from a thought or avoiding a particular worry will interfere with the process of habituation and thus maintain the anxiety that you feel. By learning to focus on one worry at a time, by worrying about it on purpose, and by sticking with the worry rather than distracting yourself, you will lower your anxiety in response to that thought.

Why Do Worry Exposure?

There are several reasons why purposely exposing yourself to your worries can be beneficial:

- Confronting your worries allows you to practice using the skills that you've learned, such as relaxation techniques or cognitive challenges to distorted thinking.

- Intentionally worrying allows you to practice focusing on one thought at a time so you can habituate to the specific worry.

- Because worry exposure decreases anxiety in response to specific thoughts, you'll be less fearful when those same thoughts arise spontaneously.

- Avoiding thoughts, or using techniques like distraction, maintains fear and can even cause more anxiety and worry. Directly confronting your worries stops that negative cycle.

How to Confront Your Worries

Effectively confronting your worries involves systematically and repeatedly facing the thoughts and images associated with specific worries. Here are the specific steps involved in worry exposure (Lang 2004; Brown, O'Leary, and Barlow 2001):

1. Develop a list of your worries

2. Create a hierarchy in which you rank these worries in order of importance, or the amount of anxiety they cause

3. Practice your imagery skills

4. Choose a worry to confront and focus on it for an extended period of time

5. Apply the anxiety management skills you learned in earlier chapters

STEP ONE: LIST YOUR WORRIES

Look back at your notebook and review the self-monitoring that you completed earlier. What worries did you identify? Do you worry about your family, your health, or your job? What do you worry might happen? If you haven't done any self-monitoring, take out your notebook now and list your most common worries. Be as specific as you can. If you have difficulty, follow the instructions in chapter 1 explaining how to monitor and record your worries. You may need to spend a few days working on this task before moving on to the next step.

STEP TWO: CREATE A HIERARCHY

Now take your list of worries and think about how much anxiety each causes you. Using a scale of 1 to 10, with 10 being the most anxiety and 1 being minimal anxiety, decide how anxious each worry makes you. Some people find rating their anxiety difficult, so don't be too concerned about the accuracy of your ratings. Just do the best you can. You can always revise your ratings later if necessary.

In your notebook, make a new list of your worries, ranked from highest to lowest anxiety. As an example, Paula's worry hierarchy might look like this:

Worry	Anxiety Rating
My kids will have unhappy lives.	*10*
My husband may get into a car accident.	*9*
My kids will fail out of college.	*8*
I may have some illness that I don't know about yet.	*8*
I don't spend enough time with my kids.	*6*
My boss will notice the mistake I made yesterday.	*5*
The bills won't get paid on time.	*5*
I'll never finish all my housework.	*4*
I'll be late for work.	*4*

STEP THREE: PRACTICE YOUR IMAGERY SKILLS

Imagining and holding a thought in your head for an extended period of time can be difficult, especially when the thought is anxiety provoking. Like any other skill, it may take time and practice to master. Many people find it easier to practice their imagery skills with scenes that are pleasant or neutral before moving on to their worry scenarios. If you have trouble visualizing the image or keeping it steadily in your mind, look back at chapter 3 and review the instructions for guided imagery. Practice with a pleasant scene prior to beginning exposure to your worrisome thoughts and images.

STEP FOUR: CHOOSE A WORRY AND CONFRONT IT

After you've created your worry hierarchy and have honed your visualization skills, it's time to pick the first worry you'll confront. To start, choose a worry that produces mild anxiety. Then write out the worst possible outcome in as much detail as you can. For Paula, it would make sense to start with her worry that she'll be late for work, since it's low on her list. She would then consider all the feared negative consequences of being late and would write them out in detail. Her worry scenario may go something like this:

> *I show up late for work and everyone notices when I walk in. My boss is standing near my desk talking to a coworker and I see him look at his watch as I walk by. I can tell that he is not pleased. He calls me into his office later that day and tells me that he cannot tolerate this kind of behavior and that it isn't fair to the other employees. He tells me that I'll have until the end of the day to clear out my desk. I'm given no time to find another job, and we can't pay our bills. We have to move out of our home and can barely afford the basic necessities of life.*

After writing out this scene, Paula would imagine it as vividly as possible. Some people find this easier to do if they record the scenario on audiotape. That way you can close your eyes and really focus on the images. The thoughts and images should be kept in mind for twenty to thirty minutes. Concentrate on them as if the scenario was actually happening. It's normal for anxiety to rise during this part of the exercise, but it should begin to decrease over the course of the exposure. Be sure to record your anxiety level in your notebook, both at the beginning of the exposure and at the end, using the 1 to 10 scale.

STEP FIVE: APPLY YOUR ANXIETY MANAGEMENT STRATEGIES

After sticking with the exposure for twenty to thirty minutes, you can apply your anxiety management techniques. For instance, Paula could identify the cognitive errors in her worry that she'll be fired for being late, she could list evidence against that belief, or she could come up with other, more likely possibilities. Relaxation techniques, such as diaphragmatic breathing, could be applied at this point as well. In your notebook, rate your anxiety again after you have used your new skills.

What to Expect During Worry Exposure

The overall effect of worry exposure will be a decrease in anxiety, but you may find that initially your anxiety is higher than normal. This is to be expected and, in fact, your anxiety *needs* to be of at least moderate intensity during the exposure period in order for the exercise to be effective. By the end of each designated exposure time, though, you should see some reduction in your anxiety from its maximum level that day. As you repeat the same worry exposure, you should see a decrease in your initial anxiety ratings from day to day. Some people also find that their anxiety tends to decrease faster the more times they repeat the exercise. Remember, you're building your endurance and working hard to increase your tolerance of these worry thoughts, so it's normal to feel physically tired or mentally fatigued. As you confront your worries, expect to feel temporarily more anxious, but if you stick with it, you should soon start to see positive results and reduced anxiety.

TIPS FOR SUCCESSFUL EXPOSURES

If you're having difficulty with the exposure exercise or if you find that your anxiety doesn't seem to be decreasing, the following strategies may help:

- Make your worry scenario as vivid and as specific as possible. Include details about the sounds, smells, sights, thoughts, and feelings involved. Write the scenario in the first person and in present tense, as if it were actually happening to you right now.

- Focus on only the present worry and keep those images in your mind without drifting to other worries or other topics. Remember that focusing on more than one worry at a time will interfere with the reduction of your anxiety.

- Be sure to stick with it! People are sometimes tempted to quit the exposure early because experiencing anxiety can be unpleasant. Often they discontinue the exercise right at the peak level of anxiety, just before it's about to subside. Stay with the image for at least thirty minutes before stopping. It only *feels* like the anxiety will never end. Hang in there—it will go down with time!

- Practice your worry exposure daily. Doing it sporadically won't work, and you will likely maintain the same high levels of anxiety. Make your efforts count! Do the exposure consistently each day.

- If you notice that your anxiety doesn't decrease, look closely for any subtle avoidance, worry behaviors, or distraction that you may be engaging in. It can be reflexive to use these types of coping strategies, but remember that they only work in the short term. In the long run, they end up maintaining your anxiety.

- Be sure to refrain from using your anxiety management skills until *after* the twenty to thirty minutes of exposure time has elapsed. Don't reassure yourself during the exposure or try to talk yourself out of the fear. The anxiety will decrease on its own.

- Use your relaxation skills and challenge your cognitive distortions after the exposure. If you have trouble generating alternative outcomes or evidence against the worry thought, ask a friend, a relative, or your therapist to help you think of some. Or, before you do the exposure exercise, try to come up with some alternatives that you can use after you've completed the exposure.

Once you've successfully practiced exposure with one of your worries and it no longer causes anxiety, it's time to move up your hierarchy. When your anxiety in response to the first worry you selected has decreased to a minimal level, start working on the next one up on your list. Use the steps above to expose yourself to this new worry until it no longer causes any anxiety. Continue to move up your hierarchy until you've confronted all your worries.

Key Points

- Avoiding worries or trying not to think about them can actually result in increased worry and anxiety.

- Worriers tend to chain several worries together, leading to escalating anxiety.

- Worry exposure involves ranking scenarios based on the anxiety they produce and then choosing one specific worry scenario to confront.

- Confronting worries one at a time allows for evaluation of the feared outcome.

- Sticking with a worry long enough results in a decrease of anxiety, or habituation.

- Worry exposure also allows an opportunity to practice applying anxiety management skills, such as relaxation skills or challenging cognitive distortions.

10 Know Your Medications

I f you've turned on the television or opened a magazine any-time recently, you've no doubt heard about the many medications now available to treat anxiety and worry. In fact, there are so many options that it may seem a bit overwhelming. Because it can be difficult to decide whether to take medications, it is important that you have accurate information to help you make the best choice. This chapter provides a basic overview of the medications that are currently available to treat anxiety. It is intended to help you discuss medication options with your physician and decide whether medication is right for you.

Not everyone who suffers from excessive worry needs medication or wants to take it. Fortunately, there are other strategies besides medication available to deal with anxiety and worry, many of which we have discussed in earlier chapters. In our practices, we have found that some anxious individuals benefit from using medication in addition to the cognitive behavioral methods described in this book, while others do fine using cognitive behavioral strategies alone. Either way, it's a good idea to learn about medication options and to consider the advantages and disadvantages of medication so that you can make an educated decision.

Advantages and Disadvantages of Medication

There are definite advantages to taking medications for your anxiety and worry. Compared to some of the cognitive behavioral exercises described in earlier chapters, taking medication requires little effort and can produce results relatively quickly. This can be appealing to people, especially when they feel overwhelmed by their anxiety or find it hard to make time to practice the cognitive behavioral skills. Medication is also widely available and can be prescribed by any knowledgeable physician, not just those specializing in anxiety. Finding a therapist who is trained in the cognitive behavioral treatment of anxiety can be more challenging than finding a physician to prescribe medication, especially outside of larger metropolitan areas. Financially, medication can be cheaper over the short term than the cost of therapy, especially if you have insurance.

Of course, there are also clear disadvantages of using only medication to address your anxiety and worry. For instance, taking medication may alleviate your anxiety symptoms to a degree, but it doesn't teach you new skills for managing anxiety. Without new skills to change your behavior and negative thoughts, reductions in symptoms from taking medications may be only temporary, and you may be vulnerable to relapse when you stop taking them. Other disadvantages of medications may include side effects and interactions with alcohol or with other medications. Medications may also negatively impact medical conditions. It is important to discuss these issues with your physician when making your decision about medication.

Medications for Anxiety and Worry

Several medications have been approved by the U.S. Food and Drug Administration (FDA) for the treatment of generalized anxiety disorder, the core feature of which is excessive worry (Goodman 2004; Albrant 1998). We've listed these medications in the table below. (We'll explain the different classes of medications a bit later in the chapter.) There are also a number of other medications that are used in the treatment of anxiety and worry that have been found to be effective as well. If you are considering trying medication to help manage your worry, you should discuss all these options with your physician.

FDA-Approved Medications for Generalized Anxiety Disorder

Medication (class)	Starting Dose (mg/day)	Daily Range (mg/day)
Venlafaxine (SNRI)	37.5	75-300
Escitalopram (SSRI)	10	10-20
Paroxetine (SSRI)	10	10-50
Alprazolam (benzodiazepine)	1	2-10
Lorazepam (benzodiazepine)	.75	3-10
Diazepam (benzodiazepine)	4	4-40
Buspirone (azapirone)	15	15-60

It's important to realize that recommended starting doses and dose ranges for medications are based on the average responses of large groups of people in research studies. There may be reasons why a dose above or below the typical starting dose or dose range makes sense in your case. For instance, factors such as hormonal influences, metabolism, and kidney or liver disease may indicate different dose requirements. If you have questions, your doctor can help you understand why a particular medication or dosage was prescribed for you.

ANTIDEPRESSANTS

Despite the name, antidepressants are actually used for a wide range of problems other than depression, including anxiety and worry. Among the different types of antidepressants, the selective serotonin reuptake inhibitors (SSRIs) are considered the first-line treatment for generalized anxiety disorder (Goodman 2004). Other categories of antidepressants, such as the serotonin-norepinephrine reuptake inhibitors (SNRIs) have been found to be effective for treating anxiety as well (Rickels et al. 2000; Sheehan 2001). Both the SSRIs and the SNRIs can take some time, typically two to four weeks, to start working. These medications are generally tolerated well, but they can cause side effects, particularly early in treatment. One side effect that's especially important for you to be aware of is that antidepressants can actually *increase* feelings of anxiety and jitteriness in the first couple of weeks. When starting an antidepressant, it helps to plan ahead for this possibility. Stress reduction and extra support may be especially helpful during this phase.

SELECTIVE SEROTONIN REUPTAKE INHIBITORS (SSRIs)

Among the SSRIs, paroxetine (Paxil) and escitalopram (Lexapro) have been approved by the FDA for the treatment of generalized anxiety disorder (Bielski, Bose, and Chang 2005). Other SSRIs, like sertraline (Zoloft), fluoxetine (Prozac), and fluvoxamine (Luvox), have also been used effectively in anxious patients (Albrant 1998). These drugs work by affecting levels of the neurotransmitter serotonin in the brain. Side effects can vary but commonly include nausea, insomnia, headache, fatigue, and sexual problems, such as decreased libido and difficulty achieving orgasm.

SEROTONIN-NOREPINEPHRINE REUPTAKE INHIBITORS (SNRIs)

The SNRI antidepressant venlafaxine (Effexor) has been found to be effective in treating anxiety as well (Sheehan 2001), and the FDA has approved it for treatment of generalized anxiety disorder. This medication affects levels of two neurotransmitters: serotonin and norepinephrine. Side effects can include nausea, dizziness, sleepiness, and sexual problems. There is also a risk of high blood pressure in some users, especially when taken in higher doses, so this should be monitored.

ANTIANXIETY MEDICATIONS

Among the antianxiety medications, there are two types proven to be effective in treating anxiety and worry: benzodiazepines and azapirones. These medications are generally helpful in treating the somatic or physical symptoms of anxiety but are possibly less effective in addressing the cognitive component of worry.

Benzodiazepines

The most well-known antianxiety medications, or anxiolytics, are in the benzodiazepine family. Benzodiazepines include drugs such as alprazolam (Xanax), lorazepam (Ativan), clonazepam (Klonopin), and diazepam (Valium), all of which have been approved by the FDA for the treatment of generalized anxiety disorder. Because they are fast acting, these medications are typically used when more immediate reduction in anxiety symptoms is needed (Sheehan 2001). These drugs are commonly used in the beginning of treatment to relieve acute distress or while waiting for another medication, like an SSRI, to take effect. But they may not be appropriate for longer-term treatment (Pollack 2001).

Common side effects include confusion or cognitive impairment, sedation, dizziness, and motor impairment. These drugs should not be used with alcohol, as the effects can be intensified or even dangerous. While many people can take these medications without incident, there is a potential for misuse, abuse, or addiction, so dosing instructions should be followed closely. Also, when discontinuing benzodiazepines, they should be tapered in a very gradual manner, and your physician should monitor you closely because there can be withdrawal symptoms, especially if the medication has been taken at high doses over a long period of time.

Azapirones

Buspirone (BuSpar) is the azapirone approved by the FDA for treating generalized anxiety disorder (Goodman 2004). Buspirone's antianxiety properties seem to come from its effect on certain receptors for the neurotransmitter serotonin. It is similar to the SSRIs in that it may take two to four weeks to show an effect. Common side effects include dizziness, light-headedness, headache, nausea, and nervousness. To be effective, buspirone must be taken two to three times per day, which can be difficult for some patients to manage.

OTHER MEDICATION OPTIONS

In addition to the medications discussed above, there are other antidepressant and antianxiety drugs as well as other types of medication that may be effective in treating anxiety and worry. These have not yet been approved by the FDA for the treatment of worry, but you can discuss them with your physician to decide if they are right for you.

Hydroxyzine

Hydroxyzine (Atarax) is an antihistamine that has been found to have some effectiveness in treating generalized anxiety disorder (Llorca et al. 2002). To see therapeutic effect, however, it may take as long as the SSRIs, or even longer. The mechanism behind its antianxiety properties is unclear but may be related to its sedative effects.

Pregabalin

Pregabalin (Lyrica) has also been found to have anxiolytic properties and has shown some effectiveness in treating generalized anxiety disorder (Pohl et al. 2005; Rickels et al. 2005). It is currently undergoing evaluation for FDA approval in the treatment of generalized anxiety disorder. It works by inhibiting the release of excess excitatory neurotransmitters via calcium channels in the central nervous system. Pregabalin is well tolerated by most patients and requires at least two doses per day.

HERBAL REMEDIES

Natural alternatives to medications are appealing to many anxious patients and have become increasingly popular in recent years. In fact, individuals who experience anxiety are among the most likely to seek alternative treatments (Kessler et al. 2001). Unfortunately, despite many claims of the benefits of herbal products, there isn't much scientific evidence to support these alternative treatments at present. These treatments are not regulated in the same way as the medications discussed earlier in this chapter. Thus, less is known about their effectiveness, dosing, side effects, or interactions with other medications.

Not enough is known yet to recommend the use of herbal products for anxiety. Any use of herbal remedies should be discussed in detail with your physician, especially if you are also taking other medications, because there may be adverse effects or interactions.

Should You Consider Medications?

The decision whether to take medications should be based on your personal preferences, knowledge of available medication options, and discussion with your physician. Here are some issues to consider in making this decision:

- How have you been doing with the exercises in this book? Have you been successful in practicing cognitive behavioral techniques? Have you noticed a reduction in your symptoms? Or have you had trouble putting the techniques to work and sticking with them?

- Do you find it difficult to cope with the physical symptoms of anxiety despite using anxiety management techniques?

- Do you have any medical conditions that may prevent you from taking medications for your anxiety?

- Are you taking any other medications that may interact with drug treatment for anxiety?

- How have you responded to any previous medications for anxiety? Do you tend to be sensitive to the side effects of medications?

- How available are other treatment options, like cognitive behavioral therapy, in your community?

Exercise: Be Prepared to Talk to Your Physician

Now that you've learned a bit about the medication options available to you and you've considered some of the issues that may be relevant in your decision, make a list of questions for your physician. Be sure to take the list to your next appointment and discuss your concerns with your doctor so that, together, you can decide on the best course of action.

Key Points

- Several medications have been approved by the FDA for treatment of generalized anxiety disorder.

- Medication has advantages and disadvantages, each of which you need to weigh carefully based on your situation.

- While herbal remedies are often touted as effective for anxiety, little research evidence is available to support these claims.

- You should always consult with your physician prior to starting any medication or herbal treatment for anxiety.

Afterword: Maintain Your Gains

After applying the solutions described in this book, you've most likely seen a significant decrease in your worry. Along the way, as you worked on controlling worry, you've also probably noticed—as we have—that worry is a challenging foe. The fight against worry is often a difficult one, filled with victories and setbacks, until your worry finally surrenders and retreats. Take a moment and congratulate yourself for gaining control over your worry. Any success you achieve is worthy of praise and celebration.

Once you've made progress in managing your worry, the next challenge you face is maintaining your gains. Sustaining your progress—and controlling your worry for life—requires four key steps: continued practice with the strategies in this book, early detection when worry returns, identifying unproductive worry, and using the solutions that worked best for you to manage new unproductive worries.

The first key step is regular practice with the solutions described in this book. Continued work with these skills and concepts will further your progress and also help prevent your worry from getting out of control again. Much like it takes regular exercise to stay in shape, it takes regular practice to keep worry under control.

It's also crucial to catch yourself as soon as you start worrying again. By recognizing worry immediately, you can act fast to regain control before it has time to take root. Some warning signs may be a return of physical symptoms caused by anxiety or more frequent negative thoughts. Early detection is crucial because when worry returns, it often does so in a different form. Recall that in the first solution described in this book, you listed your worries. However, that list represented your worries at that time. Your worries can—and most likely will—change over time. Be aware that your new worries may be completely different than the old ones. However, even though your worries may change, you can use the same techniques to manage them.

Once you recognize that you're worrying excessively again, ask yourself if your worry is productive or unproductive. Does your worry help you create possible solutions and motivate you to solve your problems? Or are you trapped in an endless web of worry, spinning around and around with no clear way out? If your worry isn't leading you toward solving your problems, it's unproductive.

If you identify your worry as unproductive, then consider your experience with this book. All of the steps described in this book are effective against worry, but not all of them are effective for everyone. Like most people, you probably found some of the solutions in this book more helpful than others. Which ones worked best for you? Record the strategies that helped you the most in your notebook. Those strategies provide the key to continued control over your worry. When—not if—unproductive worry strikes, go back to those solutions. For example, if challenging your thinking was particularly helpful, keep an eye out for new distorted thoughts. When you catch these thoughts, use the strategies in chapter 4 to untwist your thinking. If you found the relaxation techniques beneficial, practice them regularly.

When you suffer a new attack of worry, you might feel demoralized and defeated. You might be tempted to look for a new cure or a different approach to deal with worry. When worry returns, it's a common tendency to try to reinvent the wheel. Much like the perpetual dieter seeking the newest fad diet, you may find yourself seeking out new approaches to manage your worry and get back to feeling relaxed and in control. This temptation is natural. However, in most cases, the most effective approach lies in the same solutions that worked for you the first time. It's likely that these solutions will work again—with time and effort.

These four steps are the key to maintaining your progress and staying worry free for life.

If You Need Additional Help

If you find that worry is still a significant problem for you after working on the solutions described in this book, it might benefit you to seek out additional help. Finding a therapist trained in cognitive behavioral therapy and experienced with anxiety disorders might be the key to unlocking your worry. Professional organizations such as the Anxiety Disorders Association of America (www.adaa.org), the Association for Behavioral and Cognitive Therapies (www.abct.org), and the Academy of Cognitive Therapy (www.academyofct.org) can help you find a qualified therapist in your area.

Recommended Readings

Benson, H. 1975. *The Relaxation Response.* New York: HarperTorch.

Benson's classic work details the benefits of relaxation practice and describes a simple meditation technique to achieve those benefits.

Bourne, E. J. 2005. *The Anxiety and Phobia Workbook.* 4th ed. Oakland, CA: New Harbinger Publications.

This book provides an extensive collection of strategies to overcome anxiety. It contains advice on nutrition, relaxation, relationships, and more.

Burns, D. D. 1999. *The Feeling Good Handbook.* Revised ed. New York: Plume.

This popular book contains many cognitive techniques for controlling anxiety and worry.

Craske, M. G., and D. H. Barlow. 2006. *Mastery of Your Anxiety and Worry: Workbook.* 2nd ed. New York: Oxford University Press.

This workbook describes cognitive behavioral methods to help worriers learn to manage worry more effectively.

Davis, M., M. McKay, and E. R. Eshelman. 2000. *The Relaxation and Stress Reduction Workbook.* 5th ed. Oakland, CA: New Harbinger Publications.

This workbook contains detailed descriptions of effective strategies for reducing stress and achieving a state of relaxation.

Leahy, R. L. 2005. *The Worry Cure.* New York: Harmony.

The Worry Cure uses principles of cognitive behavioral therapy as well as acceptance and commitment therapy to help readers control worry.

White, J. R. 1999. *Overcoming Generalized Anxiety Disorder—Client Manual: A Relaxation, Cognitive Restructuring, and Exposure-Based Protocol for the Treatment of GAD.* Oakland, CA: New Harbinger Publications.

In White's client manual, you'll find research-proven methods for conquering worry.

References

Albrant, D. H. 1998. APhA drug treatment protocols: Management of patients with generalized anxiety disorder. APhA Psychiatric Disorders Panel. *Journal of the American Pharmaceutical Association* 38(5):543-550.

Allen, H. N., and L. W. Craighead. 1999. Appetite monitoring in the treatment of binge eating disorder. *Behavior Therapy* 30:253-272.

American Psychiatric Association. 2000. *Diagnostic and Statistical Manual of Mental Disorders.* 4th ed., text revision. Washington, DC: American Psychiatric Association.

Anxiety Disorders Association of America. 2004. New survey reveals how generalized anxiety disorder interferes with ability to maintain "healthy" relationships. www.adaa.org/aboutADAA/newsletter/newsurvey04.htm (accessed April 27, 2006).

Beck, A. T., G. Emery, and R. L. Greenberg. 1985. *Anxiety Disorders and Phobias: A Cognitive Perspective.* New York: Basic Books.

Beck, A. T., A. J. Rush, B. F. Shaw, and G. Emery. 1979. *Cognitive Therapy of Depression.* New York: Guilford Press.

Benson, H. 1975. *The Relaxation Response.* New York: HarperTorch.

Bielski, R. J., A. Bose, and C. C. Chang. 2005. A double-blind comparison of escitalopram and paroxetine in the long-term treatment of generalized anxiety disorder. *Annals of Clinical Psychiatry* 17(2):65-69.

Borkovec, T. D. 1979. Pseudo (experiential) insomnia and idiopathic (objective) insomnia: Theoretical and therapeutic issues. *Advances in Behaviour Research and Therapy* 2:27-55.

Borkovec, T. D., and E. Costello. 1993. Efficacy of applied relaxation and cognitive-behavioral therapy in the treatment of generalized anxiety disorder. *Journal of Consulting and Clinical Psychology* 61:611-619.

Borkovec, T. D., and J. Inz. 1990. The nature of worry in generalized anxiety disorder: A predominance of thought activity. *Behaviour Research and Therapy* 28(2):153-158.

Borkovec, T. D., W. J. Ray, and J. Stöber. 1998. Worry: A cognitive phenomenon intimately linked to affective, physiological, and interpersonal behavioral processes. *Cognitive Therapy and Research* 22:561-576.

Bourne, E. J. 2005. *The Anxiety and Phobia Workbook.* 4th ed. Oakland, CA: New Harbinger Publications.

Bower, S. A., and G. H. Bower. 1991. *Asserting Yourself: A Practical Guide for Positive Change.* 2nd ed. New York: Perseus Books.

Brown, T. A., T. A. O'Leary, and D. H. Barlow. 2001. Generalized anxiety disorder. In *Clinical Handbook of Psychological Disorders*, 3rd ed., edited by D. H. Barlow. New York: Guilford Press.

Burns, D. D. 1999a. *Feeling Good: The New Mood Therapy.* Revised ed. New York: HarperCollins.

Burns, D. D. 1999b. *The Feeling Good Handbook.* Revised ed. New York: Plume.

Craske, M. G., R. M. Rapee, L. Jackel, and D. H. Barlow. 1989. Qualitative dimensions of worry in DSM-III-R generalized anxiety disorder subjects and nonanxious controls. *Behaviour Research and Therapy* 27:397-402.

Dugas, M. J., K. Buhr, and R. Ladouceur. 2004. The role of intolerance of uncertainty in etiology and maintenance. In *Generalized Anxiety Disorder: Advances in Research and Practice*, edited by R. Heimberg, C. Turk, and D. Mennin. New York: Guilford Press.

Dugas, M. J., F. Gagnon, R. Ladouceur, and M. H. Freeston. 1998. Generalized anxiety disorder: A preliminary test of a conceptual model. *Behaviour Research and Therapy* 36(2):215-226.

Dugas, M. J., M. Hedayati, A. Karavidas, K. Buhr, K. Francis, and N. Phillips. 2005. Intolerance of uncertainty and information processing: Evidence of biased recall and interpretations. *Cognitive Therapy and Research* 29(1):57-70.

Dugas, M. J., and R. Ladouceur. 2000. Treatment of GAD: Targeting intolerance of uncertainty in two types of worry. *Behavior Modification* 24(5):635-657.

Ellis, A. E., and R. A. Harper. 1975. *A New Guide to Rational Living*. Hollywood, CA: Wilshire Book Company.

Foa, E. B., and M. E. Franklin. 2001. Obsessive-compulsive disorder. In *Clinical Handbook of Psychological Disorders*, 3rd ed., edited by D. H. Barlow. New York: Guilford Press.

Foa, E. B., and M. J. Kozak. 1986. Emotional processing of fear: Exposure to corrective information. *Psychological Bulletin* 99:20-35.

Goodman, W. K. 2004. Selecting pharmacotherapy for generalized anxiety disorder. *Journal of Clinical Psychiatry* 65(suppl. 13):8-13.

Jacobson, E. 1929. *Progressive Relaxation*. Chicago: University of Chicago Press.

Kessler, R. C., J. Soukup, R. B. Davis, D. F. Foster, S. A. Wilkey, M. M. Van Rompay, and D. M. Eisenberg. 2001. The use of complementary and alternative therapies to treat anxiety and depression in the United States. *American Journal of Psychiatry* 158:289-294.

Ladouceur, R., M. J. Dugas, M. H. Freeston, E. Leger, F. Gagnon, and N. Thibodeau. 2000. Efficacy of a cognitive-behavioral treatment for generalized anxiety disorder: Evaluation in a controlled clinical trial. *Journal of Consulting and Clinical Psychology* 68(6):957-964.

Ladouceur, R., P. Gosselin, and M. J. Dugas. 2000. Experimental manipulation of intolerance of uncertainty: A study of a theoretical model of worry. *Behaviour Research and Therapy* 38(9):933-941.

Lang, A. J. 2004. Treating generalized anxiety disorder with cognitive-behavioral therapy. *Journal of Clinical Psychiatry* 65(suppl. 13):14-19.

Lange, A. J., and P. Jakubowski. 1976. *Responsible Assertive Behavior: Cognitive/Behavioral Procedures for Trainers*. Champaign, IL: Research Press.

Leahy, R. L. 2003. *Cognitive Therapy Techniques*. New York: Guilford Press.

Leahy, R. L. 2004. Cognitive-behavioral therapy. In *Generalized Anxiety Disorder: Advances in Research and Practice*, edited by R. Heimberg, C. Turk, and D. Mennin. New York: Guilford Press.

Llorca, P. M., C. Spadone, O. Sol, A. Danniau, T. Bougerol, E. Corruble, M. Faruch, J. P. Macher, E. Sermet, and D. Savant. 2002. Efficacy and safety of hydroxyzine in the treatment of generalized anxiety disorder: A 3-month double-blind study. *Journal of Clinical Psychiatry* 63:1020-1027.

Lusk, J. T. 1993. *30 Scripts for Relaxation, Imagery and Inner Healing*. Duluth, MN: Whole Person Associates.

Mennin, D. S., R. G. Heimberg, and C. L. Turk. 2004. Clinical presentation and diagnostic features. In *Generalized Anxiety Disorder: Advances in Research and Practice*, edited by R. Heimberg, C. Turk, and D. Mennin. New York: Guilford Press.

Meyer, V. 1966. Modification of expectations in cases with obsessional rituals. *Behaviour Research and Therapy* 4:273-280.

Pohl, R. B., D. E. Feltner, R. R. Fieve, and A. C. Pande. 2005. Efficacy of pregabalin in the treatment of generalized anxiety disorder: A double-blind, placebo-controlled comparison of BID versus TID dosing. *Journal of Clinical Psychopharmacology* 25(2):151-158.

Pollack, M. H. 2001. Optimizing pharmacotherapy of generalized anxiety disorder to achieve remission. *Journal of Clinical Psychiatry* 62(suppl. 19):20-25.

Rapp, J. T., R. G. Miltenberger, E. S. Long, A. J. Elliott, and V. A. Lumley. 1998. Simplified habit reversal treatment for chronic hair pulling in three adolescents: A clinical replication with direct observation. *Journal of Applied Behavior Analysis* 31:299-302.

Rickels, K., M. H. Pollack, D. E. Feltner, R. B. Lydiard, D. L. Zimbroff, R. J. Bielski, K. Tobias, J. D. Brock, G. L. Zornberg, and A. C. Pande. 2005. Pregabalin for treatment of generalized anxiety disorder: A 4-week multicenter double-blind placebo-controlled trial of pregabalin and alprazolam. *Archives of General Psychiatry* 62(9):1022-1030.

Rickels, K., M. H. Pollack, D. V. Sheehan, and J. T. Hawkins. 2000. Efficacy of extended-release venlafaxine in nondepressed outpatients with generalized anxiety disorder. *American Journal of Psychiatry* 157:968-974.

Rossman, M. L. 2001. *Guided Imagery for Self-Healing: An Essential Resource for Anyone Seeking Wellness.* 2nd ed. Tiburon, CA: H. J. Kramer.

Sheehan, D. V. 2001. Attaining remission in generalized anxiety disorder: Venlafaxine extended release comparative data. *Journal of Clinical Psychiatry* 62(suppl. 19):26-31.

Steketee, G. 1993. *Treatment of Obsessive-Compulsive Disorder.* New York: Guilford Press.

Stöber, J., and J. Joorman. 2001. Worry, procrastination, and perfectionism: Differentiating amount of worry, pathological worry, anxiety, and depression. *Cognitive Therapy and Research* 25:49-60.

Van Eerde, W. 2003. Procrastination at work and time management training. *Journal of Psychology* 137(5):421-434.

Wegman, D. 1994. *White Bears and Other Unwanted Thoughts: Suppression, Obsession, and the Psychology of Mental Control.* New York: Guilford Press.

Wells, A. 1999. A cognitive model of generalized anxiety disorder. *Behavior Modification* 23(4):526-555.

Zinbarg, R. E., M. G. Craske, and D. H. Barlow. 1993. *Mastery of Your Anxiety and Worry: Therapist Guide.* San Antonio, TX: Harcourt Brace.

Kevin L. Gyoerkoe, Psy.D., is codirector of the Anxiety and Agoraphobia Treatment Center in Chicago and Northbrook, IL. He is assistant professor at the Chicago Professional School of Psychology, a certified fellow of the Academy of Cognitive Therapy, and a member of the Scientific Advisory Board of the Obsessive-Compulsive Foundation of Metropolitan Chicago.

Pamela S. Wiegartz, Ph.D., is assistant professor of clinical psychology at the University of Illinois at Chicago, where she teaches courses on CBT, directs the Obsessive-Compulsive Disorders Clinic, and maintains a practice dedicated to treating individuals with anxiety disorders. She has published numerous peer-reviewed journal articles and book chapters on the treatment of anxiety, is a certified fellow of the Academy of Cognitive Therapy, and a member of the Scientific Advisory Board of the Obsessive Compulsive Foundation of Metropolitan Chicago.

more **simple solutions** to real challenges
from new**harbinger**publications

10 SIMPLE SOLUTIONS TO PANIC
How to Overcome Panic Attacks, Calm
Physical Symptoms & Reclaim Your Life

$11.95 • Item Code: 3252

10 SIMPLE SOLUTIONS TO SHYNESS
How to Overcome Shyness, Social
Anxiety & Fear of Public Speaking

$12.95 • Item Code: 3481

WOMEN WHO WORRY TOO MUCH
How to Stop Worry & Anxiety
from Ruining Relationships, Work & Fun

$13.95 • Item Code: 4127

CALMING YOUR ANXIOUS MIND
How Mindfulness & Compassion Can
Free You from Anxiety, Fear & Panic

$12.95 • Item Code: 3384

COPING WITH ANXIETY
10 Simple Ways to Relieve Anxiety,
Fear & Worry

$12.95 • Item Code: 3201

 available from new**harbinger**publications
and fine booksellers everywhere

To order, call toll free **1-800-748-6273** or visit our online bookstore at **www.newharbinger.com**
(V, MC, AMEX • prices subject to change without notice)